GOVERNMENT PROCEDURES AND OPERATIONS

STATES' REDUCTIONS OF UNEMPLOYMENT BENEFITS

CIRCUMSTANCES AND IMPLICATIONS

GOVERNMENT PROCEDURES AND OPERATIONS

Additional books in this series can be found on Nova's website under the Series tab.

Additional e-books in this series can be found on Nova's website under the e-book tab.

GOVERNMENT PROCEDURES AND OPERATIONS

STATES' REDUCTIONS OF UNEMPLOYMENT BENEFITS

CIRCUMSTANCES AND IMPLICATIONS

ELIAS HOFFMAN
EDITOR

nova publishers
New York

Library of Congress Cataloging-in-Publication Data

ISBN: 978-1-63483-980-8

Published by Nova Science Publishers, Inc. † New York

CONTENTS

Preface		**vii**
Chapter 1	Unemployment Insurance: States' Reductions in Maximum Benefit Durations Have Implications for Federal Costs *United States Government Accountability Office*	**1**
Chapter 2	Unemployment Insurance: Consequences of Changes in State Unemployment Compensation Laws *Katelin P. Isaacs*	**67**
Index		**93**

PREFACE

As part of the nation's unemployment insurance (UI) system, overseen by DOL, states provide benefits to eligible unemployed workers, with additional weeks of benefits sometimes provided by the federal government in times of economic stress. Since the 1960s, states have had maximum UI benefit durations of 26 weeks or longer. However, since 2011, nine states have reduced their maximum benefit durations. This book examines the circumstances in which states reduced the maximum duration of UI benefits; the implications of these reductions for individuals; the effects on federal UI costs; and their broader economic effects. Furthermore, the book analyzes recent changes to state Unemployment Compensation (UC) programs.

In: States' Reductions of Unemployment Benefits ISBN: 978-1-63483-980-8
Editor: Elias Hoffman

Chapter 1

UNEMPLOYMENT INSURANCE: STATES' REDUCTIONS IN MAXIMUM BENEFIT DURATIONS HAVE IMPLICATIONS FOR FEDERAL COSTS*

United States Government Accountability Office

ABBREVIATIONS

AHCM	average high cost multiple
BLS	Bureau of Labor Statistics
CBO	Congressional Budget Office
CRS	Congressional Research Service
DOL	Department of Labor
FUTA	Federal Unemployment Tax Act
GDP	gross domestic product
SSDI	Social Security Disability Income
TTR	Total Taxable Resources
UI	unemployment insurance

* This is an edited, reformatted and augmented version of a Congressional Research Service publication GAO-15-281 , prepared for Members and Committees of Congress, dated April 2015.

Why GAO Did This Study

As part of the nation's UI system, overseen by DOL, states provide benefits to eligible unemployed workers, with additional weeks of benefits sometimes provided by the federal government in times of economic stress. Since the 1960s, states have had maximum UI benefit durations of 26 weeks or longer. However, since 2011, nine states have reduced their maximum benefit durations: Arkansas, Florida, Georgia, Illinois, Kansas, Michigan, Missouri, North Carolina, and South Carolina. GAO was asked to review the states' reductions.

GAO examined (1) the circumstances in which states reduced the maximum duration of UI benefits, (2) the implications of these reductions for individuals, (3) the effects on federal UI costs, and (4) their broader economic effects. GAO reviewed relevant federal and state laws; visited Georgia and Michigan, which had different approaches to reducing durations; analyzed UI program data from 2006 (before the recession) to 2014; and reviewed relevant economic research.

What GAO Recommends

GAO recommends that the Secretary of Labor examine the implications of state duration reductions for federal UI program costs and develop recommendations, if warranted. DOL agreed with GAO's recommendation and indicated it will begin to assess an approach for studying the implications of reductions in maximum duration on federal costs.

What GAO Found

The unemployment insurance (UI) system, a federal and state partnership that provides benefits to eligible workers who have lost their jobs, was under financial pressures during the recent recession and recovery. Since 2011, nine states reduced the maximum length of time (duration) individuals could receive state benefits. These states reduced duration from 26 weeks to as few as 12 weeks, with 20 weeks being the most common new maximum. Compared to states that did not reduce duration, those that did generally had higher unemployment rates and weaker UI trust fund balances and were more likely to have federal loans as their UI reserves became depleted. Officials in five of the nine states said that replenishing their trust fund balance was a key rationale for reducing benefit duration. GAO found that most of the nine states, like other states, also increased employer taxes for their UI program and made other benefit reductions such as by changing UI eligibility rules.

Reductions in state benefit durations resulted in some individuals receiving substantially less in total UI benefits. During the period from 2009 through 2013, individuals who exhausted their state benefits could receive additional weeks of benefits from the federal government. The duration of federal benefits was based on the duration of state benefits; shorter maximum state benefit periods resulted in shorter maximum federal benefit periods. As a result, some individuals received substantially less in total UI benefits because the durations of both their state and federal benefits were reduced. For example, in 2013, an individual in a state that had shortened its maximum benefit duration to 20 weeks could have received up to 52.4 additional weeks of federal benefits, for a total of 72.4 weeks. However, had the state maximum duration remained at 26 weeks, that individual could have received up to 67 weeks of federal benefits, for a total of 93 weeks. In contrast, individuals eligible for UI benefits for relatively short periods of time were unaffected by the reduced durations.

The effects of these reductions on federal UI program costs are unclear. Although GAO's prior work on past recessions found it can be useful for federal agencies to assess the unintended consequences of state policy responses, the Department of Labor (DOL) has not assessed the extent of any cost shift to the federal government. The net impact on federal UI costs would depend on how reductions in the duration of state benefits affect the number of people receiving federal benefits and for how long. On the one hand, federal costs are increased to the extent that state duration reductions shift individuals to federal benefits earlier. On the other hand, federal costs are decreased to the extent that fewer weeks of federal UI benefits are available. However, because DOL has not analyzed state data on individuals' weekly benefits, it remains unclear whether the federal government incurred a net cost due to the states' duration reductions.

Relevant research suggests that reductions in benefit duration may reduce the positive effects of UI on the economy. The economic literature that GAO reviewed, including analysis by the Congressional Budget Office, generally indicates positive macroeconomic effects from the UI program, based on the likelihood that benefits are spent, thus providing a stimulus to the economy.

April 22, 2015
The Honorable Patty Murray
Ranking Member
Committee on Health, Education, Labor, and Pensions
United States Senate

The Honorable Jack Reed
United States Senate

The recent recession and the slow recovery placed extraordinary demands on the nation's unemployment insurance (UI) system—a program of temporary wage replacement. UI benefits are generally provided through states and extended, at times, with federally-provided benefits, for example during periods of high unemployment.[1] Between late 2007, when the recession began, and early 2009, the total dollar value of state-funded UI benefit payments to individuals increased 164 percent nationwide and 22 states experienced increases of 200 percent or more.

The UI system provides temporary benefits that partially replace earnings for individuals who have lost jobs through no fault of their own. Under federal law, there is no minimum or maximum period of time state programs must provide benefits. From the 1960s until recently, according to the Congressional Research Service (CRS), all states provided benefits up to 26 weeks, and 2 states provided additional weeks. During periods of high unemployment, the federal government has provided UI benefits beyond the states' maximum durations. Since 2011, however, 9 states reduced the maximum allowable duration for their benefits:

Arkansas, Florida, Georgia, Illinois, Kansas, Michigan, Missouri, North Carolina, and South Carolina. Among these states, the most common new maximum duration is 20 weeks, and in 2 states it can be as low as 12 weeks under certain conditions.

You asked us to review state reductions in maximum durations to assess their significance. Our review examines (1) the circumstances in which states reduced the maximum duration of their UI benefits to fewer than 26 weeks, (2) the implications of these reductions for individual UI claimants in these states, (3) the effect, if any, on costs for the federal government, and (4) what is known about the broader economic effects of these benefit reductions.

To identify the circumstances in which states reduced the maximum duration of state unemployment benefits, we reviewed relevant federal laws and regulations, as well as relevant state laws, interviewed federal UI program officials and state UI officials in 7 of the 9 states that reduced their durations,[2] and conducted site visits to 2 of them—Georgia and Michigan. We selected these 2 states because they differed in type, magnitude, and timing of the duration reductions, as well as geographic region. In the site visit states, we conducted additional interviews with selected state legislators, researchers, governors' workforce policy advisors, employer groups, and labor advocates. To understand more broadly how state UI programs responded to challenges following the recession, we also interviewed state UI officials in 4 states that did not reduce their UI benefit duration. We selected 3 of these states—Indiana, Ohio, and Tennessee—based on their similarity to the states that reduced benefit duration. We selected the fourth state, Washington, on the basis of expert recommendation. To identify state characteristics that most distinguished the states that reduced duration from those that did not, we analyzed data for all 50 states and the District of Columbia,[3] primarily from the Department of Labor's (DOL) Office of Unemployment Insurance and Bureau of Labor Statistics (BLS). The data analyzed included both UI program and financing characteristics, as well as state demographic and economic characteristics. We also analyzed these data to address potential implications of duration reduction for individuals, focusing on the 9 duration reduction states and the 4 states we selected that did not reduce duration.

To examine any potential effect of the states' maximum duration reductions on costs to the federal government, we analyzed data provided to us by two states, Georgia and Missouri. These data included specific items from reports that states provide regularly to DOL. We assessed the reliability of the data we used for this report.[4] In each case, we collected information about the data series in question, such as the uses of the data, applicable internal controls, and data entry practices. We determined the data to be sufficiently reliable for the purpose of this report. Finally, we reviewed economic literature to understand the significance of UI benefits for individuals, in terms of their attachment to the labor force and job search behavior, among other implications, and the effects of UI on the economy. From this research, we derived reasonable conclusions about the likely implications of duration reductions for individuals and the broader economic effects of these benefit reductions. For additional information about our methodology, see appendix I.

We conducted our work from November 2013 through April 2015 in accordance with generally accepted government auditing standards. Those standards require that we plan and perform the audit to obtain sufficient, appropriate evidence to provide a reasonable basis for our findings and conclusions based on our audit objectives. We believe the evidence obtained provides a reasonable basis for our findings and conclusions based on our audit objectives.

BACKGROUND

UI: A Federal and State Partnership

The nation's UI system is a joint federal/state partnership originally authorized by the Social Security Act and funded primarily through federal and state taxes on employers. Under this arrangement, states administer their own programs, generally known as regular UI benefits, according to certain federal requirements and under the oversight of DOL's Office of Unemployment Insurance. The primary objectives of this partnership are to provide temporary, partial compensation for lost earnings to individuals who have become unemployed through no fault of their own and to help stabilize the economy during economic downturns.[5]

Federal law sets forth broad provisions for the categories of workers who must be covered by the program, some benefit provisions, the federal tax base and rate, and program administration, such as how states will repay any funds they borrow from the federal government to pay benefits when state reserves are depleted.

States have considerable flexibility to set benefit amounts and their duration, or the maximum period of time that the state pays benefits, and establish eligibility requirements and other program details.[6] Regarding duration, for example, most states provided up to 16 weeks in 1938, after the program was first established.[7] More recently, states provided up to 26 weeks.[8] In the wake of the recession, according to DOL, 9 states reduced benefit duration, with 20 weeks—representing a reduction of over 20 percent—the most common new maximum (see table 1).[9] Among these states, 4 enacted new maximum durations that vary according to the state's unemployment rate (referred to in this report as "variable duration"), while the other 5 states' new maximum durations do not vary in this way (referred to in this report as "flat duration"). All 9 states established these new durations through changes in state law.[10]

Table 1. States That Reduced the Maximum Duration of Unemployment Insurance Benefits to Fewer Than 26 Weeks Since 2011

State	Maximum benefit duration before reduction (weeks)	New maximum benefit duration (weeks)	Year duration reduction[a] enacted
Arkansas	26	25	2011
Florida[b]	26	12-23	2011
Georgia[b]	26	14-20	2012
Illinois[c]	26	25	2011
Kansas[b]	26	16-26	2013
Michigan	26	20	2011
Missouri	26	20	2011
North Carolina[b]	26	12-20	2013
South Carolina	26	20	2011

Source: DOL, Comparison of State Unemployment Laws, selected years, and GAO analysis of relevant state laws. | GAO-15-281

[a] In some states, the date that the change took effect was later than the enactment date.

[b] In these states, the maximum duration varies within the range shown, depending on the state's total unemployment rate. For example, in Kansas, 26 weeks of benefits are available only when the total unemployment rate in the state is 6 percent or more. According to state officials, as of October 2014, the maximum duration in Kansas was 20 weeks.

[c] Illinois' reduction to 25 weeks was temporary, and applicable to claims filed in 2012. Illinois law also sets forth a future temporary reduction to 24 weeks, which will be applicable to claims filed in 2016 and 2018. 820 Ill. Comp. Stat. 405/403 (2014).

States also have flexibility to establish eligibility requirements, which can affect duration.[11] There are two kinds of eligibility requirements. Monetary eligibility typically refers to an earnings threshold and employment history that applicants must meet in order to qualify for benefits. Based on such eligibility criteria, individuals may qualify for less than a state's maximum duration.[12] The other category of eligibility requirements is non-monetary, which according to DOL, refers to states' criteria to determine if an individual's job loss is through no fault of his or her own,[13] and that the individual is able to work, available for work, and actively seeking work. According to DOL, each state's law sets both monetary and non-monetary requirements for eligibility.

Federal Programs Can Provide UI Benefits Beyond the State Maximum

In addition to the state UI benefits, federal emergency and extended UI programs may sometimes provide additional weeks of benefits under certain economic conditions, such as rising unemployment or economic downturns.

Temporary Federal UI Programs. During economic downturns, Congress has sometimes passed legislation to provide temporary unemployment compensation. Most recently, such a temporary program was created by the Supplemental Appropriations Act, 2008 (Emergency Unemployment Compensation; "emergency benefits" for the purposes of this report).[14] According to CRS, this represented the eighth time a federal temporary unemployment compensation program was created since the inception of the UI program. This program provided up to 53 additional weeks of emergency benefits to qualifying claimants and expired in December 2013.[15] After establishing the recent emergency benefits program in 2008, Congress amended the program 11 times, extending it and in some cases adding weeks of benefits, according to information provided by DOL. From December 2008 until the program expired in December 2013, emergency benefits were available in all states, including the states that reduced duration, with the exception of North Carolina (see app. V).[16]

Extended UI Benefits. In addition, states and the federal government provide "extended" benefits to workers. This program, which has no expiration date, provides up to 13 additional weeks of benefits to workers who have exhausted state unemployment insurance benefits during periods of high unemployment.[17] According to CRS, some states have also utilized an option to pay up to 7 additional weeks of extended benefits when unemployment reaches certain levels. While financing for extended UI benefits is typically shared between the states and the federal government, the American Recovery and Reinvestment Act of 2009, as amended, provided for temporary full federal funding of the extended benefits program through December 2013.

According to DOL, from January 2009 to May 2013, 39 states met the criteria for extended benefits at various times, including all of the states that reduced duration, and since May 2013, no state has met the criteria for federal extended benefits (see app. V). During the recovery, the maximum period for all combined benefits—state, emergency, and extended—to qualifying claimants reached 99 weeks in some states (see fig. 1).[18]

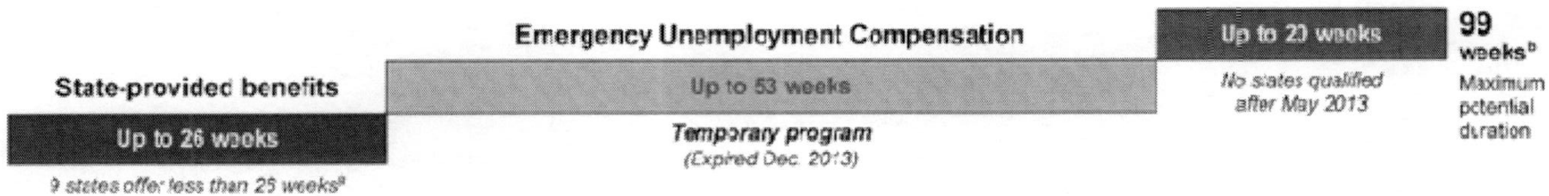

Source: GAO presentation of Congressional Research Service data. | GAO-15-281.

[a] In most states, the maximum duration remains 26 weeks.

[b] According to CRS, total potential maximum duration for all programs reached 99 weeks between November 8, 2009 and September 1, 2012, but was 93 weeks when the emergency program expired in December 2013.

Figure 1. Sequence of Unemployment Benefits by Unemployment Programs.

Calculating Federal Benefits

Under both emergency and extended benefit programs, the duration of an individual's federal UI benefits has depended, in part, on the duration of his or her state UI benefits. If a claimant was entitled to fewer than 26 weeks of state benefits, the duration of any available federal benefits to the claimant would be reduced proportionally. Under the most recent rules for the emergency program, the formula specified that, for the first level or "tier" of benefits, benefits were payable for up to 54 percent of the duration of an individual's total state benefits.[19] Extended benefits can provide up to 50 or 80 percent of the duration of an individual's total state benefits, depending in part on the rate of unemployment in the claimant's state. For the 80 percent level to be applicable, a state must have a provision in its laws causing extended benefits to become available when the unemployment rate reaches a certain level. Both federal emergency and extended benefits were available in 2011, when duration reductions were first enacted in 6 states (see fig. 2).

UI Financing

The UI program was designed to be forward funded[20] and self-financed by states through a trust fund that the federal government maintains on behalf of the states.[21] Ideally, states build reserves in their trust fund accounts through revenue from employer taxes during periods of economic expansion in order to pay UI benefits during economic downturns. Because unemployment can vary substantially during a business cycle, it is important that states build sufficient reserves so trust fund balances remain solvent during recessions.

The UI program is financed primarily by state taxes levied on employers, as well as a federal tax—the Federal Unemployment Tax Act (FUTA) tax—also levied on employers.[22] Employers receive a FUTA tax credit depending on the extent to which their state UI programs comply with federal criteria. Specifically, states set a taxable wage base—the maximum amount of an employee's wages subject to UI employer taxes—and any wages above this amount are not subject to taxation. In addition, states determine the employer tax rate levied on the taxable wage base. In order for employers in a state to qualify for the full FUTA tax credit, the state's taxable wage base must at least be equal to the FUTA wage base—currently $7,000. In addition, the state's tax rate for each employer may vary according to the employer's layoff records—a practice known as experience rating.[23] Experience rating results in lower tax rates for employers with fewer layoffs and higher tax rates for those with more layoffs.[24] States can also levy other taxes on employers, known as surtaxes or surcharges, for various purposes.

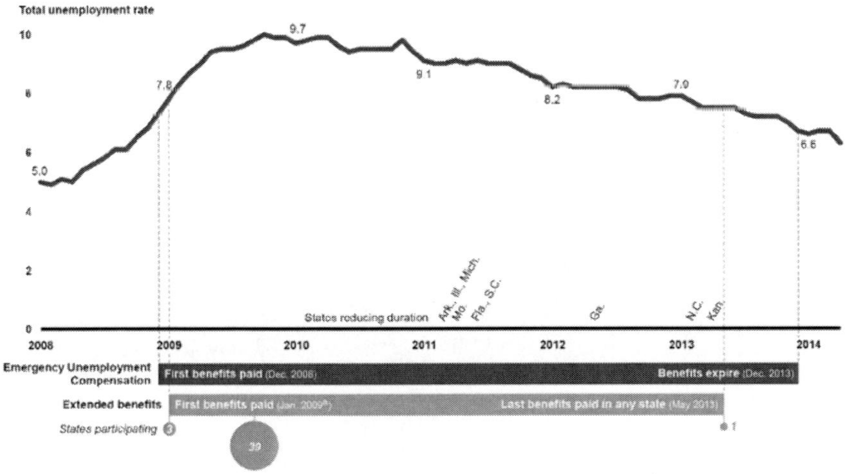

Source: Department of Labor and Congressional Research Service. | GAO-15-281.

Note: The unemployment rate declined in the recovery but so did labor force participation.

[a] This figure represents the period when Extended Benefits were first paid during the most recent recession.

Figure 2. Changes in Unemployment Benefits and Nation's Unemployment Rate, 2008-2014.

In addition to their ability to change tax rates, states can make changes to program benefits to help ensure that funds are available to pay future benefits. For example, as previously mentioned, states can change program eligibility provisions to limit or expand the population who qualify for benefits. States can also change benefit amounts directly.[25] Figure 3 shows the various tools states generally use to balance program revenue and benefits.

Although states have flexibility to change both revenues and benefits, they can exhaust their UI reserves during periods of exceptional unemployment. In such times, states may borrow from the federal government. If a state satisfies certain conditions, loans taken from January 1 through September 30 and repaid before October 1, are interest free as long as the state does not borrow again during the fourth quarter of the calendar year. In states that do not repay their loans within a specified period, employers lose a portion of the FUTA tax credit.[26] However, states with outstanding loans can still seek relief from these loan provisions in the form of a limit to the reduction of the FUTA tax credit and the opportunity to delay interest payments.[27] During the recent recession, most states opted to borrow from the federal government: 36 states had federal trust fund loans, and the total borrowed reached $48.5 billion in March 2011.[28] As of March 2015, 9 states and the U.S. Virgin Islands had trust fund loan balances, totaling about $14 billion.

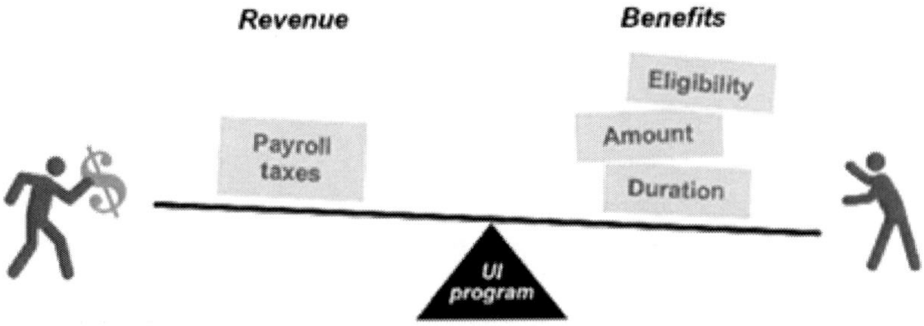

Source: GAO. | GAO-15-281.

Figure 3. Balancing Unemployment Insurance Program Revenue and Benefits.

Measures of UI solvency are expressed as a percentage of wages, typically total annual wages earned by employees who are potentially eligible for receiving UI benefits. Among the measures that DOL reports are reserve ratios[29] and the high cost multiple.[30] A high cost multiple measure of 1.0 corresponds to sufficient reserves to pay benefits at the high cost rate for 1 year without taking in additional revenue, according to DOL. A similar measure is the average high cost multiple (AHCM), which divides a trust fund's reserve ratio by the average high cost rate, which uses a multi-year average.[31] An AHCM measure of 1.0 is the target for solvency, recommended by the Advisory Council on Unemployment Compensation and is specified in DOL regulations providing for interest-free loans.[32] States also monitor their own trust fund balances. We have previously reported that almost all states measure their trust fund balances and make tax rate changes once per year.[33] According to our previous report, the majority of states have trust fund balance targets written into their state laws, with triggers built in to adjust the tax rates according to the balance. Most states impose higher tax rates when their trust fund balances are low and lower rates when their balances are high, according to DOL.

States That Reduced UI Benefit Durations Generally Had Weak Pre-Recession Trust Funds and Raised Taxes While Improving Solvency

In our analysis of the 9 duration reduction states, we found that as a group they exhibited several characteristics that tended to distinguish them from other states.[34] Overall, as compared to the states that did not reduce duration, the states that reduced duration had:

- weaker trust fund balances before the recession;
- lower total taxable resources;
- federal loans to a greater degree;
- higher unemployment rates;
- lower union membership rates; and
- greater political homogeneity.

In addition, while state officials cited a range of considerations in reducing benefit durations, we found that most duration reduction states, like most of the states we selected for comparison that did not reduce duration, raised taxes and made other changes to their programs. Overall, our interviews with state officials could not establish the degree to which any characteristics or considerations affected the decisions to reduce durations.

Duration Reduction States Generally Had Weaker Finances and Faced Higher Unemployment Rates than States That Did Not Reduce Duration

Weaker Trust Fund Balances

Duration reduction states were more likely than other states to enter the recession with trust fund balances that were inadequate to pay historical benefit levels. Specifically, 8 of the 9 duration reduction states (89 percent) had an AHCM below 1.0 in the last quarter of 2007—indicating an inadequate trust fund balance—as compared to 25 of the 42 states (60 percent) that did not reduce duration. Duration reduction states had a median AHCM of .33, which was less than half the median AHCM of .79 among states that did not reduce duration (see fig. 4). Consequently, the trust fund balances of the duration reduction states were particularly vulnerable to recessionary pressures and these states faced a greater risk of depleting their trust fund balances than states with more adequate trust fund balances. Among the states that reduced duration and among those that did not, there was variation in AHCM values: for example, as shown in figure 4, 1 duration reduction state among the 9 did have an adequate AHCM. In contrast, 17 of the 42 states that did not reduce duration had an AHCM greater than 1.[35]

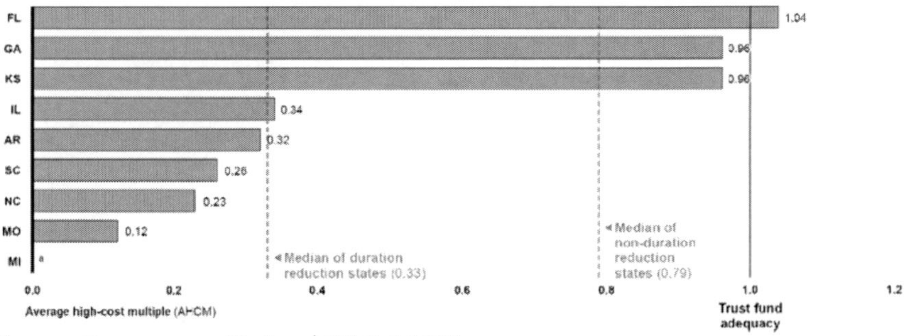

Source: Department of Labor. | GAO-15-281.

Figure 4. Unemployment Insurance Trust Fund Adequacy before the Recession: Average High Cost Multiple for Duration Reduction States, 4th Quarter 2007.

The inadequacy of trust fund balances may have been a factor in the decision to reduce duration for some states. Officials from 5 of the 7 duration reduction states with whom we had interviews cited the condition of their state's trust fund balance as having been a likely consideration in the decision to reduce duration.[36] One state UI director said it had been a driving factor in his state's deliberation.

The weak or inadequate trust fund balances may have been partially a result of relatively low employer UI tax rates. Specifically, 5 of the 9 reduction states had average UI tax rates on total wages that were lower than the U.S. average for the 5 years preceding reduction.[37] Additionally, stakeholders in 4 reduction states told us that there were periods (prior to the recession) of up to several years in which employer UI taxes were held to minimal levels through means such as tax holidays, tax cuts, actions to suppress automatic tax adjustment mechanisms, and actions to distribute some trust fund revenues to employers.[38] We have previously reported that long-standing UI tax policies and practices in many states have eroded trust fund reserves, leaving states in a weak position prior to a previous recession.[39]

Lower Total Taxable Resources

Additionally, duration reduction states had weaker overall fiscal capacity than other states. The total taxable resources of duration reduction states were generally lower than those of states that did not reduce duration, according to a measure of states' overall fiscal capacity calculated by the Department of the Treasury.[40] In 2010 (the year before any duration reductions occurred), 8 of the 9 duration reduction states had measures of total taxable resources below the median per capita indexed value for the U.S. overall, and 3 of these states had measures that were among the lowest in the country (see app. II for more information).[41]

More Likely to Have Federal Trust Fund Loans

States that reduced their benefit durations were more likely to have received a federal trust fund loan since 2010 (see app. II for more information). Specifically, all 9 duration reduction states took such loans at some point during the recession; whereas 61 percent of nonreduction states had trust fund loans (see app. II for the maximum trust fund loan balances for each state). While the size of loans varied among reduction states, 2 of them (Michigan and North Carolina) ranked among the top 4 states nationwide with the largest debt per covered employee.

Higher Unemployment Rates

States that reduced UI benefit duration also tended to have higher unemployment rates. Before they adopted duration reduction, almost all— 7 of 9—duration reduction states had total unemployment rates of 9 percent or more.[42] In contrast, 14 of 42 states that did not reduce duration—one-third—had unemployment rates of 9 percent or more in 2010. Higher unemployment rates increase the pressure on UI trust funds because they reflect the population of those who could qualify for and receive UI benefits.

Lower Union Membership Rates

Duration reduction states also had lower rates of union membership. In 2010, 7 of the 9 duration reduction states had rates of union membership below the median for states that did not reduce duration—13.2 percent— and 3 of them had rates that were among the 5 states with the lowest rates in the country—5.6 percent or lower. Low union membership has been associated with lower benefits and wages in the economics literature.

Greater Political Homogeneity

Finally, duration reduction states also exhibited fairly homogenous political composition of their legislatures and governorships, which may have facilitated development and adoption of the state laws that included duration reduction. We found that 8 of the 9 duration reduction states had a single party in control of both the legislature and the governorship when reductions were enacted.[43] In contrast, 45 percent of nonreduction states were politically homogeneous in 2010, although by 2013, this was the case for 71 percent.

State Officials Cited Some Additional Factors Relevant to Reducing Benefit Durations

Beyond the characteristics that tended to distinguish the states that reduced duration from other states, officials in some duration reduction states suggested other considerations as influential. Specifically, officials cited a federal program requirement and the availability of federal benefits, among other reasons for reducing duration.

In 4 of the 7 states where we interviewed UI officials, officials cited the federal nonreduction requirement as a possible factor. This requirement made states that directly reduced UI benefit amounts ineligible for federal UI emergency funds, thereby limiting the range of options available to states to reduce benefit costs.[44] As one state official said, this rule suggested that "no other effort to reduce benefits [beyond reducing duration] would be acceptable."

Also, although the duration reductions will continue regardless of the availability of federal benefits, in 4 of the 7 states where we interviewed UI officials, officials said the availability of federal benefits may have played a role in the decision to reduce the maximum duration of state-funded benefits. The availability of federal benefits meant that claimants would generally continue to receive benefits, albeit federal benefits, beyond the new maximum state duration. One state UI official told us the state's reduction was "not significant," in part because federal benefits were then available, and another told us that the legislature likely anticipated minimal impact on claimants. In 7 of the 9 duration reduction states, the total maximum duration of all available benefits, including federal benefits, was at least 93 weeks at the time of duration reduction (see app. V).

During our interviews, officials in 2 states cited the state's economic health and the need to encourage claimants' reemployment efforts as reasons for reducing duration. Specifically, officials in Kansas said that duration in that state is tied to the health of the state's economy so that longer durations are available when the unemployment rate is high. Kansas is 1 of 4 states, along with Florida, Georgia, and North Carolina, that adopted variable maximum durations. They provide more weeks of benefits when the total state unemployment rate is high, and fewer weeks when it is low (see app. III).

Duration Reduction States Raised Taxes and Made Other Program Changes

States reduced maximum benefit duration in the context of other changes to their UI programs, according to information provided by state officials and our review of selected state laws. Some of these changes, such as tax increases, played a role in repaying federal loans and improving their trust fund balances.[45] States also made other changes to their programs that can reduce benefit payments, such as changes related to eligibility and program integrity.

Increasing Tax Revenues. Of the 9 duration reduction states, 7 adopted increases in employer taxes, some of them temporary, according to information provided by state officials.[46] Specifically, these states changed the taxable wage base, employer tax rates, supplemental taxes, or some combination of these (see app. III).

Data provided by the states suggest that tax increases likely played a greater role than benefit duration reductions in repaying loans and restoring solvency. Notwithstanding the relatively small savings associated with duration reductions in most states, four employer groups told us there was a need to balance the increased revenue from employers with some sacrifice on the claimant side, and characterized duration reductions as providing such a balance.[47] To understand the relative role of duration reductions and tax increases, we asked the states whether they had estimated any cost savings associated with duration reductions. Of the 7 duration reduction states we contacted, 4 provided estimates of cost savings equivalent to 3.4 percent, 4.6 percent, 9.8 percent, and 44.9 percent of their maximum loan balances (see app. III).[48] In addition, officials in the 3 other duration reduction states we contacted identified tax changes as among the actions that contributed most to repayment of the trust fund loan, and one of these states identified duration reduction as a major contributor to repaying the loan. One official estimated that state tax rate changes accounted for about 65 percent of the funds needed to restore the trust fund balance.

Other Changes. Two duration reduction states issued bonds to repay their loans.[49] On the benefits side, one state lowered its benefit amount, according to CRS.[50] In addition, 8 of the 9 duration reduction states made changes to program eligibility. These included changes to requirements for individuals regarding earnings or employment history, as well as changes to rules addressing conduct for which an individual could be disqualified. In one state, eligibility changes were enacted to reverse previous expansions of eligibility under federal law, such as eligibility for those who claimed UI on the basis of part-time employment.[51]

Actions taken to address program integrity were reported by all 7 of the 9 duration reduction states that provided information, and included activities to address overpayments, detect fraud, and impose penalties for noncompliant employers.[52] State officials reported that these actions were taken in response to both federal and state initiatives.

Comparison States Also Made Program Changes but Varied in Consideration of Benefit Duration

The 4 states we examined that did not reduce duration also reported making similar program changes in raising employer taxes, tightening eligibility, and strengthening program integrity. Specifically, 3 of the 4 comparison states reported increasing employer taxes. Of the 3 comparison states that had loans, two— Indiana and Tennessee— reported increasing employer taxes (see app. III).[53] The third state with a loan, Ohio, was considering changes to its UI program, including to employer taxes.[54] The fourth state, Washington, did not require a loan, and officials told us that the state's taxable wage base—the maximum amount of an employee's wages subject to tax—was raised through a provision in state law that took effect automatically, while employer taxes were reduced.

Regarding eligibility, 3 of the 4 comparison states reported recent actions to tighten eligibility, such as by strengthening work requirements.[56] All states reported taking actions to strengthen program integrity, such as efforts to address overpayments.

The 4 comparison states varied in the extent to which they considered reducing maximum duration. Indiana, Ohio, and Tennessee were similar to the duration reduction states, for example, in terms of having had weak trust fund balances before the recession.[56] However, UI officials in Indiana told us that benefit amounts for some claimants had already been reduced in 2011, and no further actions have been taken on the benefit side. In Ohio, which has a large outstanding loan balance, state UI officials told us that a bipartisan group of legislators was considering changes to the program, including a potential reduction in maximum duration. Officials in Tennessee and Washington told us that duration reduction had not been considered in their states.[57]

REDUCTION IN MAXIMUM DURATION OF UI BENEFITS LOWERED TOTAL BENEFITS FOR SOME INDIVIDUALS

Reduced Durations Decreased Total Benefits for Some Individuals

In the duration reduction states, those UI claimants who would have been eligible to receive benefits beyond the new maximum receive less in total benefits in the absence of federal UI programs. The foregone benefit for those individuals who would have exhausted benefits under the previous duration can be estimated as the product of the number of weeks of the reduction and the average weekly benefit amount. For example, Michigan had an average weekly benefit of $273 in the third quarter of 2014 and the maximum benefit duration was 20 weeks (a reduction of 6 weeks from the previous maximum). A claimant in Michigan who would have been eligible for 26 weeks of benefits absent the reduction could receive 20 weeks of benefits. The claimant's foregone benefit can be estimated as $1,638 (or 6 times the average weekly benefit amount). Benefits foregone by individuals in the states whose durations do not fluctuate with unemployment rates (flat maximums) ranged from $289 to $1,638 (see table 2)

As expected, foregone benefits would vary for individuals who would have exhausted benefits under the previous duration in the 4 states where maximum durations are tied to the unemployment rates —Florida, Georgia, Kansas, and North Carolina. The benefit amount foregone by individuals in these states ranged from $1,370 to $2,926 (see table 3.)

Table 2. Foregone Unemployment Benefit Amounts per Claimant in Duration Reduction States with Flat Maximum Durations, as of 2014

States with flat maximum duration[a]	New state maximum duration (weeks)	Previous duration (weeks)	Average weekly benefit 2014 Q3	Foregone benefit amountfor claimants who wouldhave been eligible for 26weeks of state UI benefits
Arkansas	25	26	$289	$289
Michigan	20	26	$273	$1,638
Missouri	20	26	$238	$1,428
South Carolina	20	26	$252	$1,512

Source: GAO analysis of relevant state law, information provided by states, and information provided by the Center on Budget and Policy Priorities. | GAO-15-281.

[a]While Illinois reduced duration to a flat 25 week maximum, that reduction was only applicable to claims filed in 2012.

Table 3. Foregone Unemployment Benefit Amounts per Claimant in Duration Reduction States with Variable Maximum Durations, as of October 2014

States with variable maximum duration	New maximum duration range (weeks)	Previous maximum duration (weeks)	New maximum duration as of October 2014	Average weekly benefit 2014 Q3	Foregone benefit amountfor claimants who wouldhave been eligible for 26weeks of state UI benefits
Florida	12-23	26	16	$137	$1,370
Georgia	14-20	26	15	$266	$2,926
Kansas	16-26	26	20	$348	$2,088
North Carolina	12-20	26	14	$227	$2,724

Source: GAO analysis of relevant state law, information provided by states, and information provided by the Center on Budget and Policy Priorities. | GAO-15-281.

One potential rationale for tying maximum durations to the unemployment rate is that a lower unemployment rate signals that more jobs are available and, consequently, a shorter UI duration may be sufficient to find employment. In such a scenario, UI claimants may find jobs sooner and may not be affected by the decreased maximum duration. On the other hand, improvement in the unemployment rate is not the only factor that affects unemployment levels—

lower unemployment rates can be caused in part by individuals giving up the job search altogether and dropping out of the labor force.

Some state UI directors told us their states examined the average duration on UI when legislators were considering where to set the new maximum durations. For example, Georgia officials told us that average duration had been below 14 weeks for years, and was recently closer to between 11 and 13 weeks. On the other hand, average duration on UI does not always reflect the average length of unemployment for several reasons—for example, an unemployment spell can exceed the maximum weeks of UI benefits. When we examined the average length of unemployment for persons in these states, we found that it is generally longer than the state's new maximum benefit duration.[58] In the states that reduced duration, the average length of unemployment for all unemployed persons—not just those receiving UI—for 2014 ranged from almost 24 weeks to nearly 44 weeks. The maximum durations in these states ranged from 14 to 25 weeks, as of October 2014 (see table 4).

Table 4. Average Length of Unemployment and Maximum Unemployment Benefit Duration in States that Reduced Duration, as of October 2014

State[a]	Average length of unemployment, 2014 (weeks)	Maximum duration, October 2014 (weeks)	Difference betweenaverage length ofunemployment andcurrent maximumduration (weeks)
Arkansas	23.6	25	-1.4
Florida	43.7	16	27.7
Georgia	38.6	15	23.6
Kansas	25.1	20	5.1
Michigan	37.1	20	17.1
Missouri	31.4	20	11.4
North Carolina	35.7	14	21.7
South Carolina	31.2	20	11.2
All states (average)	30.8	26[b]	4.8

Source: GAO analysis of relevant state laws, information provided by states, the Bureau of Labor Statistics, and the Center on Budget and Policy Priorities. | GAO-15-281

[a] While Illinois reduced maximum duration to 25 week maximum, that reduction was only applicable to claims filed in 2012.

[b] For states that did not reduce duration.

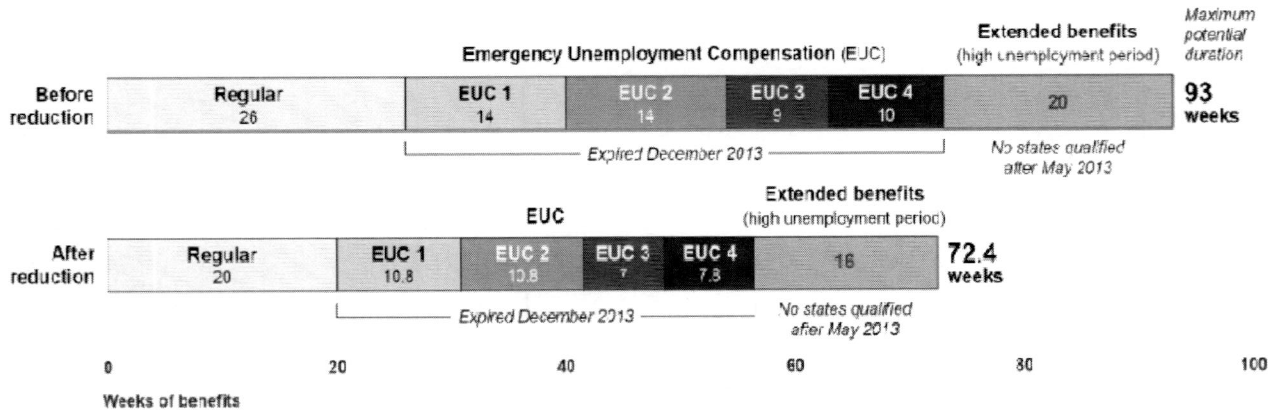

Source: GAO presentation of Congressional Research Service data amd review of relevant federal law. |GAO-15-281.

Figure 5. Potential Maximum Duration of State and Federal Unemployment Insurance Benefits, Assuming a Reduction of State Benefits to 20 Weeks, as of May 2013.

When federal UI benefits were in effect (most recently generally from 2009 until the end of 2013),[59] those individuals who were eligible to receive UI benefits for the *maximum* total state and federal duration would have received substantially less benefits following reduction, since duration in each federal benefit program depends, in part, on the duration of state benefits. Specifically, in a state that reduced benefits from 26 to 20 weeks, those claimants who would have received state and federal benefits for up to 93 weeks before the reduction would receive benefits for up to 72.4 weeks after the reduction, as illustrated in figure 5.

However, UI benefit durations would not change for those claimants who would have received benefits for less than 72.4 weeks before the reduction. For example, prior to any reductions in maximum benefit durations, an individual who found employment after 36 weeks of receiving UI benefits would have received 26 weeks of state benefits and 10 weeks of federal emergency unemployment benefits. All else equal, such an individual would have still received a total of 36 weeks of benefits in a scenario in which the state reduced maximum duration, for example, to 20 weeks, although the source of the benefit would change: 20 weeks of state benefits and 16 weeks of federal emergency unemployment benefits (see fig. 6).

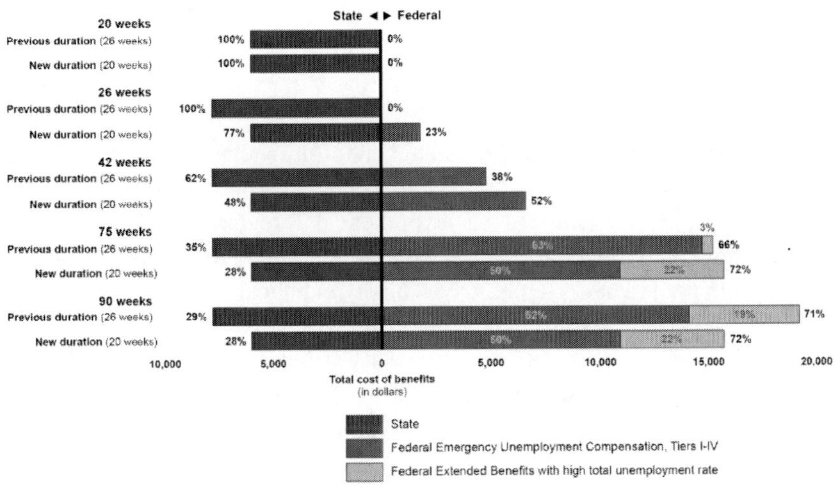

Source: GAO analysis of Congressional Research data. | GAO-15-281.

Figure 6. Unemployment Insurance Benefits Paid at Shorter Unemployment Durations, Assuming State Reduced Maximum Duration from 26 to 20 Weeks, as of December 2013.

Estimating the Numbers of Affected Individuals

Because DOL does not collect data at the individual level, we were not able to quantify the number of individuals affected by duration reduction. To estimate the number of individuals who would be affected by a duration reduction, as well as other potential effects, we asked officials in Washington state to prepare an estimate using the state's benefit financing model. Although Washington State did not reduce duration, its model was developed to help analysts project the condition of their UI trust fund balance several years into the future and allow the state to assess the financial impact of various economic scenarios and possible legislative changes. The model showed that if maximum duration in Washington was reduced from 26 weeks to 20 weeks, at an average weekly benefit amount of $389, over 32,000 additional individuals would have exhausted their benefits in 2013, when federal benefits were in effect, representing a 46 percent increase in exhaustions. In addition, unemployed individuals in the state would have collectively foregone nearly $117 million in benefits in that year—a 9.5 percent decrease in state benefits. Appendix IV has more details on the simulation and the model.

Source: GAO analysis of information provided by Washington State Employment Security Department. | GAO-15-281.

To illustrate how reductions in state benefit durations could have affected UI claimants who were eligible to receive benefits for the maximum state and federal durations, we calculated a hypothetical foregone benefit amount to illustrate how the reduction in state maximum duration could impact benefits paid through the federal programs. For this hypothetical scenario (for example in May 2013), we assume that a claimant was eligible for the maximum benefit duration available, and that 20 weeks of federal extended benefits and all four tiers of emergency benefits were in effect, although this was not the case in all states. In such a scenario, hypothetical foregone benefits could range from around $700 to over $20,000 (see table 5).[60]

Table 5. Hypothetical Foregone Unemployment Benefit Amounts in Duration Reduction States Assuming 93 Weeks of Total Benefits before Duration Reduction, as of May 2013

	New state maximum duration (weeks)	*Previous maximum duration with federal benefits[a] (weeks)*	*New maximum duration with federal benefits (weeks)*	*Average weekly benefit 2013 Q2[b]*	*Hypotheticalforegone benefitamount*
States with flat maximum duration					
Arkansas	25	93	90.5	$289	$723
Michigan	20	93	72.4	$297	$6,118
Missouri	20	93	72.4	$240	$4,944
South Carolina	20	93	72.4	$247	$5,088
States with variable maximum duration					
Florida	12-23	93	43.4 – 83.3	$234	$2,270 –$ 11,606
Georgia	14-20	93	50.7 – 72.4	$265	$5,459 –$11,210
Kansas	16-26	93	57.9 – 93	$339	$0 –$11,892
North Carolina[c]	12-20	93	12-20[c]	$301	$21,973 –$24,381

Source: GAO analysis of relevant state and federal law, information provided by states, and information provided by the Center on Budget and Policy Priorities. | GAO-15-281

[a] From November 8, 2009 to September 1, 2012, as much as 99 weeks of benefits was available; however, from September 2012-December 2013, 93 weeks was the maximum available, according to the Congressional Research Service. Although not all states would have qualified for these amounts as of May 2013, according to data provided by DOL, this chart assumes that states have chosen extended benefits for a high unemployment period and that states qualify for all four tiers of emergency unemployment benefits, and that 93 weeks is the maximum available.

[b] This is the last quarter in which states qualified for federal extended unemployment benefits.

[c] Because North Carolina reduced benefit amounts, it was not eligible for federal emergency compensation after reduction, according to the Congressional Research Service.

Shorter Benefit Durations Reduce Household Spending and May Not Hasten Reemployment

In light of our findings that some individuals may have received less total UI benefits due to duration reduction, we also examined research on the impact of decreases in UI benefits on individuals.[61] The literature we reviewed considered the theoretical basis for and empirical research on the implications for individuals of changes in UI benefits (amounts and duration) in terms of labor market behavior, poverty, and enrollment in social safety net programs.

Theories of economic efficiency generally propose that the ideal UI benefit amount and duration would prevent sharp reductions in the claimant's household spending without creating incentives for an unnecessarily lengthy job search. Benefits that are too high prolong job searches and can elevate unemployment, while benefits that are too low reduce spending during jobless spells and cause workers to accept suboptimal employment.

According to the research, some claimants facing shorter UI benefit durations may find employment, while others may leave the labor force.[62] Some models show that a longer benefit period—and thus a longer job search—can result in better job offers that enable workers to be more productive, although empirical support for this possibility is limited. Nevertheless, with low or unavailable benefits, research has found that some people give up on seeking employment and leave the labor force altogether. Unemployment benefits promote labor force participation, both on the "front end' by reducing the layoff risk in work covered by UI, and on the "back end" in the event of layoff, by reducing labor force exit.

In our own work, some of the state UI directors and stakeholders we interviewed told us that they hoped reduced benefit duration would increase reemployment. However, the available research on UI duration and claimants' reemployment offers little support to the premise that reducing duration increases reemployment. In an economy with few jobs relative to the number of job seekers—as was the case during the recession and the slow recovery when the ratio of job seekers to job openings rose to as much as six to one—a shorter benefit period is not likely to return individuals to the labor force sooner. One study estimated that as many as one-third of claimants who exhaust benefits are unable to find work. [63] However, it is difficult to determine with more certainty how many people do or do not find jobs once they stop receiving benefits because of limited data on individuals who have left the program.

Empirical research indicates longer durations prolong spells in the program. However, the implication of longer spells for the overall unemployment rate is ambiguous. Shortened durations could lead to reemployment, but the reemployed UI claimant might have taken a job otherwise obtained by someone outside the program. Alternatively, shorter durations could also lead to earlier exit from the labor force. Lengthened durations could lead to longer spells in the program, but also, with the benefit of more search time, to the program participant finding a job for which they are better suited. Studies that specifically consider net employment for the entire labor force indicate little effect from shorter benefit durations. For the same reason, research finds that shorter durations have a negative effect on consumption in families of unemployed workers, since shorter benefit durations do not necessarily result in rapid reemployment.[64]

Some research finds that reduced benefits—including those resulting from reduced durations—lead to a greater incidence of poverty among those eligible for UI benefits. UI has been shown to reduce poverty; the Census Bureau estimated that UI benefits kept 1.2 million people out of poverty in 2013.[65] Another recent study found that UI reduced the poverty rate among unemployed workers from 22.5 percent to 13.6 percent.[66]

Studies are inconclusive as to whether reduced UI benefits result in more people seeking assistance from federal benefit programs such as Social Security Disability Insurance (SSDI), Supplemental Security Income, Temporary Assistance for Needy Families, and the Supplemental Nutrition Assistance Program (formerly known as food stamps).[67] For example, a 2010 study found that UI extensions reduce SSDI claims,[68] while a 2013 study found no relation between benefit exhaustion and disability claims.[69] However, longer benefit durations may delay applications that would eventually be made to other programs, such as SSDI.

We examined UI program and economic indicators, and found that, on average, individuals in reduction states were less likely to participate in UI and more likely to leave the labor force than individuals in nonreduction states. Additionally, while the rates at which claimants exhausted their UI benefits increased during the recession, and declined since 2010, these rates were consistently higher in duration reduction states on average as compared to states that did not reduce duration. Although duration reductions may have affected some of these indicators, it is difficult to attribute causation, given the many other program changes made by the states and federal government, as well as the changes occurring in the economy. For more information on our analysis of individual states, see appendix V.

DURATION REDUCTION BY STATES SHIFTED SOME COSTS FROM STATES TO THE FEDERAL GOVERNMENT

In the presence of federal UI benefit programs, reducing maximum state UI benefit durations affects federal program costs in two opposing ways. First, at the front end, claimants use federal benefits earlier than they would have absent a state reduction, so the federal government pays some costs that states otherwise would have paid. For example, in states that reduced the maximum duration of state UI benefits from 26 weeks to 20 weeks, those claimants who were eligible for benefits for more than 26 weeks transitioned to federal benefits 6 weeks earlier. In addition, federal benefits were paid to some claimants who would not have received any federal benefits absent the reduction. Specifically, in states that reduced duration to 20 weeks, federal benefits were paid to any eligible claimants who exited the program during weeks 21 through 26.

Second, at the back end, federal benefits were not available for as long as they would have been absent a reduction in state durations, which potentially led to some federal savings. For example, claimants could receive up to 67 weeks of federal benefits when the maximum state benefit duration was 26 weeks. After a reduction to 20 weeks, those claimants could receive a maximum of 52.4 weeks of federal benefits.[70] As a result, some of the upfront costs that were shifted to the federal government in weeks 21 through 26 are offset by shorter federal benefit durations at the back end, as shown in table 6.

The net cost to the federal government due to the reduction in state benefit durations is difficult to measure because the amount and duration of federal program benefits depend on both a claimant's state benefits and how long he or she is eligible.[71] For example, we found that before duration reduction, a claimant who received benefits for 75 weeks—26 weeks of state benefits and 49 weeks of federal benefits—would receive fewer total weeks of benefits after reduction in state duration to 20 weeks, but more weeks of federal benefits. Specifically, the claimant would receive 20 weeks from the state, and then 52.4 weeks of federal benefits, providing a total of 72.4 weeks of UI benefits. (See fig. 7.)

Table 6. Sample Effect on Federal Unemployment Insurance Programs of Reducing Maximum State Benefit Duration from 26 to 20 Weeks, as of May 2013

Prior to reduction, Benefit weeks cost paid by:		After reduction, cost paid by:	Changes in cost to federal government (per claimant)
1 20	State	State	0
21 - 26	State	Federal government	+ 6 weeks of benefits
27 - 72.4	Federal government	Federal government	0
72.4 - 93	Federal government	Eliminated by reduction	-20.6 weeks of benefits

Source: GAO analysis of relevant federal law and Congressional Research Service reports. | GAO-15-28.

Note: For this table, we assume that 20 weeks of extended benefits and all four tiers of emergency benefits are in effect, and that the federal government pays the full cost of extended benefits.

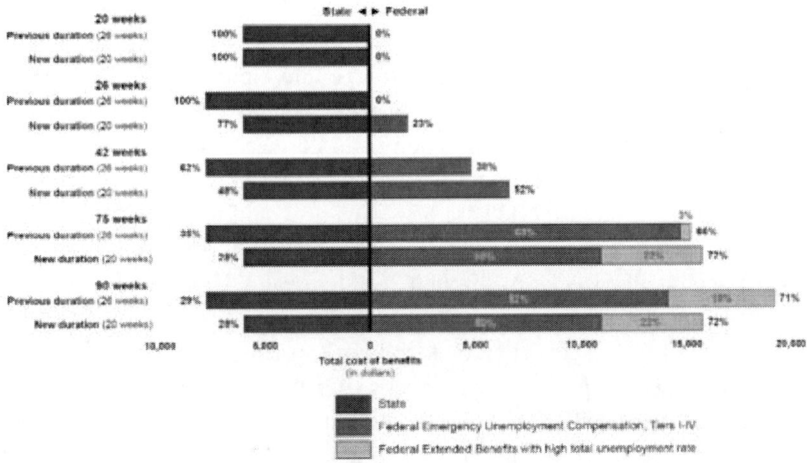

Source: GAO analysis of Congressional Reseach data. | GAO-15-281.

Note: Because federal UI program benefit durations have been tied to state UI benefit durations, total benefits (state and federal combined) would be available for a maximum of 72.4 weeks in a state that had a 20 week maximum. Our analysis assumes that the federal government pays all extended benefits, as was the case in May 2013, the last month in which any state qualified for extended benefits.

Figure 7. State and Federal Costs at Selected Unemployment Benefit Durations, Assuming State Reduced Duration from 26 to 20 Weeks, as of May 2013.

Over time, some claimants find jobs or exit the program for other reasons. As a result, there are likely to be fewer claimants receiving benefits at the back end of the program than during the front end. Therefore, even though state duration reductions may have resulted in fewer weeks of federal benefits, costs to the federal government may have increased. In other words, the front end cost caused by an earlier transition to federal programs by more claimants may exceed any savings generated by paying fewer weeks of federal benefits to those claimants still receiving benefits at the back end of the federal programs.

It is difficult to measure the magnitude of the front end costs and back end savings because, while DOL collects aggregate data on benefits paid, it does not collect data on weekly benefits at the individual level. Nevertheless, using data provided by two states, Missouri and Georgia, we found that the earlier transition to federal benefits shifted some costs from these states to the federal government.

In order to illustrate the front end cost shift to the federal government for one calendar year quarter for the weeks from the end of state benefits through week 26, for example, we analyzed data from Missouri and Georgia on the number of claimants who received weekly benefits, by benefit week.[72] For each benefit week beyond the new state maximum duration, we multiplied the number of claimants by the average weekly benefit amount in each state. Missouri reduced its maximum duration from 26 weeks to 20 weeks effective April 2011. Using the average weekly benefit amount for claimants in Missouri, we calculated the federal government would have paid about $23.7 million in benefits for one calendar year quarter for the claimants who received benefits for weeks 21 through 26.[73] See figure 8 for estimated costs to federal programs for the first 6 weeks after reduction.

Whether front end costs to the federal government were offset by back end savings generated by paying fewer weeks of benefits depends on the amount the federal government would have paid in the weeks eliminated by the reduction in state benefit durations. Specifically, if the federal cost of UI benefits for weeks 72.4 through 93 exceeds $23.7 million, then the federal government would have realized cost savings by paying benefits for weeks 21 to 26 while eliminating benefits in weeks 72.4 through 93. Conversely, if the federal cost of benefits for weeks 72.4 through 93 is less than $23.7 million, then the federal government would have realized cost increases as a consequence of the state duration reduction.[74]

Similarly, Georgia reduced its benefit duration from 26 weeks to a variable duration of 14 to 20 weeks, effective July 1, 2012. Using the average weekly benefit amount for claimants in Georgia, and assuming a maximum duration of 18 weeks, we calculated that the federal government would have paid about $27.2 million in benefits that the state would previously have paid for the claimants who received benefits for weeks 19 through 26, as shown in figure 9.

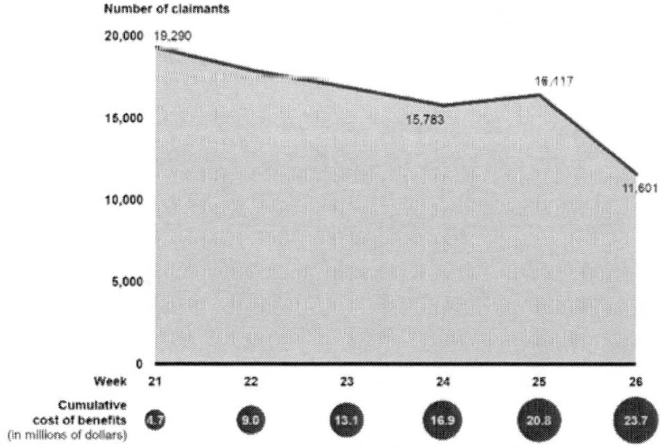

Source: GAO analysis of Mission and Department of Labor data. | GAO-15-281.

Figure 8. Estimated Costs to the Federal Government after Missouri's Unemployment Benefits Duration Reduction, Weeks 21-26.

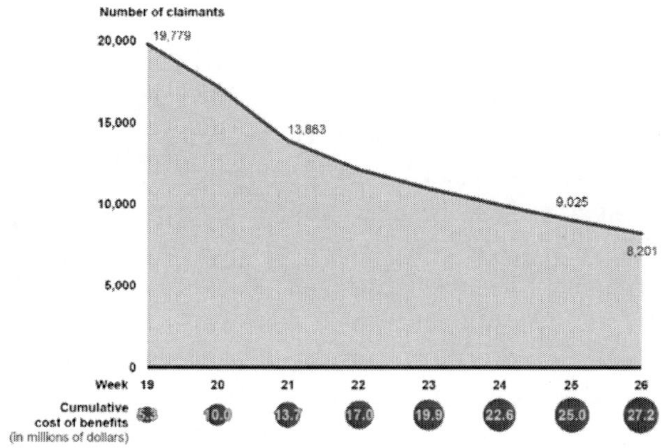

Source: GAO analysis of Georgia and Department of Labor data. | GAO-15-281.

Note: Estimated costs reflect data on actual number of claimants and average weekly benefit amounts for the quarter before duration reduction.

Figure 9. Estimated Costs to the Federal Government after Georgia's Unemployment Benefits Duration Reduction, Weeks 19-26.

Our analysis of these 2 states shows that there could be a net cost shift to the federal government, perhaps unintended, as a result of state duration reductions. As we have previously reported on state policy changes in past recessions, knowledge of the unintended consequences of such changes—including estimates of the impact on federal costs—can inform federal assistance to states in future recessions.[75] Additionally, in our report on best practices in estimating costs, we have noted that cost estimates should identify and reflect budgetary uncertainties.[76] However, DOL has not assessed the extent to which state duration reductions, adopted by states in the wake of the recent recession, affected costs to the federal government. To do so would require an analysis of weekly benefit data for individuals, which are collected by the states, and not by DOL. Without an analysis of the cost implications of duration reductions, DOL and Congress lack information needed to plan for future economic downturns and the equitable role of the federal government in the federal/state UI partnership.

RESEARCH SUGGESTS THAT REDUCTIONS IN BENEFIT DURATION MAY LESSEN UI'S POSITIVE EFFECTS ON THE ECONOMY

The relevant economic literature on UI that we reviewed, including analysis by the Congressional Budget Office (CBO), considers the benefits to be a source of economic stabilization, by increasing aggregate demand through a "multiplier effect" during downturns. The multiplier effect is derived from claimants' tendency to spend a high proportion of their benefits. The maximum duration of state benefits has not varied substantially since the 1960s, according to CRS.[77] We reviewed the research that focuses on maximum durations of benefits (federal and state benefits combined). To the extent benefits are reduced, such as by a shortened benefit period, the effects on gross domestic product (GDP) and employment are likely to be negative, although the precise magnitude would be difficult to determine.[78]

Research on the stimulus effects of spending has generally focused on estimates of the "multiplier" effect, in this case for UI benefits (see sidebar). An increase in UI benefits is an increase in income to claimants, who are likely to spend a high proportion of these benefits. The multiplier effect captures the effects of this initial spending, as well as the subsequent stream of spending by other parties. The UI claimant spends benefits, and those who benefit from this spending, in turn, increase their own spending, and so on. The sum total of all such ripple effects is embodied in estimates of a multiplier associated with the initial spending increase. Effects of changes in individual states' duration could have less pronounced effects than national changes.

Experts provide varying estimates of the extent to which an increase in government spending causes those whose incomes are directly benefited, such as the unemployed, to increase their own spending, and by extension increase aggregate demand and GDP. However, estimates of the multipliers in the short term are almost always positive. Responding in 2011 to a proposed extension of UI benefits, CBO estimated multipliers for UI of between .4 and 1.9 using a model that draws from multiple schools of thought, including leading models used by other institutions, related to proposed extensions of UI benefits.[79] A private sector estimate also found a positive effect. In 2012, investment firm Moody's estimated the multiplier for UI to be 1.55, also in relation to proposed extensions of benefits.[80] Both estimates found that the multiplier for UI is generally higher than those for other types of spending, such as reductions in payroll taxes for workers and employers.[81]

Multiplier Effect

A multiplier effect represents the expansion in GDP or employment related to some change in public spending or taxes. A multiplier is a way of showing the economic impact of a dollar as it moves through the economy. For example, a multiplier of 1.5 means that an increase in spending by $1 (financed by borrowing) expands GDP by $1.50. | GAO-15- 281

Similarly, some recent studies have estimated the effect on GDP and employment of UI benefit terminations, as decreases in benefits can also have ripple effects. In 2013, for example, the Council of Economic Advisors and DOL used private-sector and CBO estimates to determine that discontinuation of federal emergency benefits could reduce GDP by .2 to .4 percentage points.[83] This report also estimated that terminating these federal benefits could result in a potential loss of 240,000 jobs. Additionally, in December 2011, using a CBO multiplier, the Joint Economic Committee estimated that continuing federal benefits could generate up to 400,000 jobs overall.[84]

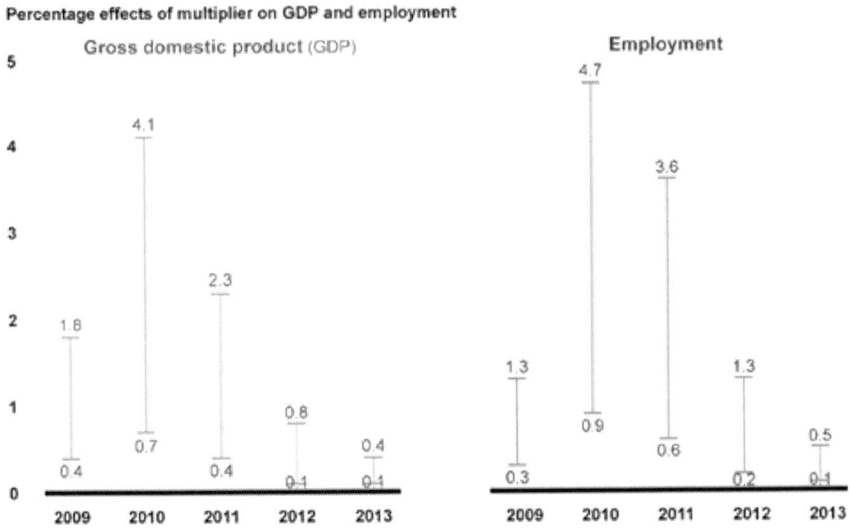

Source: GAO analysis of Congressional Budget Office data. | GAO-15-281.

Notes: Employment data reflect percentage multiplier effect in terms of full-time equivalent employment years. The American Recovery and Reinvestment Act of 2009 included both extensions of UI benefits as well as other measures that can stimulate the economy, such as Medicaid financing and surface transportation funding. Although CBO did not estimate multipliers for the UI extensions separately, they are likely to exhibit the same pattern.

Figure 10. Congressional Budget Office Estimates of the Maximum and Minimum Multiplier Effects for Stimulus Provisions of the American Recovery and Reinvestment Act of 2009.

Identifying any effects from 9 states' duration reductions on the economy as a whole would be complicated by potentially offsetting factors. For example, the effect of a spending decrease in one program, in this case, UI, could be mitigated by a spending increase in another program, because multipliers work in both directions.

Furthermore, experts disagree on the extent to which an increase in government spending may provoke offsetting behavior by other entities, based on our review of relevant literature. For example, UI claimants may spend their benefits, but taxpayers may reduce their spending in anticipation of higher taxes to service government debt, canceling the intended stimulus effect.[85]

With regard to the role UI plays in stabilizing the economy during economic downturns, the program stands out as an important component of the federal government's automatic stabilizers. It avoids the shortcomings of other types of fiscal stimulus because it is highly targeted to individuals with low income and a high likelihood of spending the benefits, and it is timely because it promptly increases in periods of rising unemployment and falls as the economy recovers.[86]

CONCLUSION

The joint federal and state unemployment partnership provides temporary financial relief to individuals who have become unemployed through no fault of their own, and stabilizes the economy during economic downturns. While states determine the amount and duration of benefits paid to individuals through unemployment insurance, their decisions have an impact on the federal government's role and costs. In the recent recession and slow recovery, 9 states chose to reduce the maximum duration of benefits paid to individuals and, as previously mentioned, none of the states that we interviewed reported any restoration of the previous maximum duration. As we have shown, these states' actions will lead to reductions in total benefits for some claimants. If total benefits were reduced, the UI program's objectives to provide relief to unemployed individuals and help stabilize the economy during downturns would be adversely affected.

The states' decisions to reduce benefit durations reflect the flexibility afforded states that can help them make adjustments appropriate to their particular circumstances during challenging economic times. In addition, a larger federal role during downturns is consistent with the part that UI plays as an economic stabilizer. Yet the state duration reductions also had the unintended consequence of recasting the federal role—causing the federal programs to fund weeks of benefits that were formerly the responsibility of states.

Further, these costs were shifted to the federal government without necessarily providing more weeks of total benefits for the individual. DOL does not have information about the costs shifted to the federal government and about the changes in total durations resulting from the states' actions. As we have previously reported on state policy changes in past recessions, knowledge of the unintended consequences of such changes—including estimates of the impact on federal costs— can inform federal assistance to states in future recessions.

Without an analysis of the extent to which costs were shifted to the federal government as a result of state duration reductions, the agency and Congress lack information needed to plan for future economic downturns and the equitable role of the federal government in the federal/state unemployment insurance partnership.

Recommendation for Executive Action

To inform the design of any future federal UI programs, the Secretary of Labor should examine the implications of state reductions in maximum UI benefit duration on federal UI costs, for example, by modeling the net effect of paying federal benefits earlier to more beneficiaries, albeit for a possibly shorter period of time, and develop recommendations for the program, if appropriate.

Agency Comments and Our Evaluation

We provided a draft of this report to DOL for review and comment. In its written comments, DOL agreed with our recommendation. Specifically, DOL noted that additional study would be useful, and indicated it will begin to assess an approach for determining the implications of reductions in maximum duration on federal costs. DOL noted that measuring the net cost to the federal government is difficult, and we acknowledge this difficulty. However, understanding the federal cost associated with state duration reductions will inform any proposed modifications to the UI federal-state partnership and the balance of costs.

DOL noted that it has proposed incentives to states to maintain maximum durations of 26 weeks, included in the President's fiscal year 2016 budget. For example, one proposal would make several changes to the extended benefits program, including providing 100 percent federal funding for states with 26-week maximum durations. DOL also provided technical comments, which we incorporated as appropriate.

Additionally, we provided selected state UI agencies with a draft of pertinent sections and incorporated their technical comments as appropriate.

We also asked an external expert to review the report, and made technical changes based on this review as appropriate.

Andrew Sherrill
Director,
Education, Workforce, and Income Security Issues

APPENDIX I: OBJECTIVES, SCOPE, AND METHODOLOGY

To address the objectives of this request, we used a variety of methods. Specifically, we

- reviewed relevant federal laws and regulations and state laws, and confirmed information regarding state laws with relevant state officials;
- interviewed federal unemployment insurance (UI) program officials and state UI officials in 7 states that reduced duration and 4 states that did not reduce duration, and in 4 of the 7 states that reduced duration, we also interviewed other stakeholders with an interest in UI duration, such as employer groups and advocates;
- conducted a cluster analysis using data from the Department of Labor's (DOL) Office of Unemployment Insurance, the Bureau of Labor Statistics (BLS), and other sources;
- analyzed data on a range of variables using data from DOL and BLS;
- calculated survival rates (the probability that a claimant will continue receiving benefits after a given week) based on data provided to us;
- conducted an economic literature review on key implications of UI benefits for individuals; and
- conducted an economic literature review that focused primarily on the stimulative effects of UI, and identified reasonable conclusions about the likely economic effects of duration reduction.

Interviews of Federal and State UI Officials and Other Stakeholders

To identify the circumstances in which states reduced the maximum duration of state benefits, we interviewed federal UI program officials and state UI officials in 7 of the 9 states that reduced duration and 4 states that did not reduce duration (Indiana, Ohio, Tennessee, and Washington). We selected Indiana, Ohio, and Tennessee based on their similarity to the duration reduction states on certain criteria, including presence of a trust fund loan and the size of the loan; geographic location; average high cost multiple; total taxable resources; and total unemployment rate. In addition, we selected Washington on the basis of expert recommendation and mention in selected studies. Washington was among a minority of states that did not require a federal UI trust fund loan at any point during the recession and recovery. The UI officials in Florida and North Carolina did not respond to our questions. We also conducted site visits to two duration reduction states—Georgia and Michigan—where we interviewed a wide range of stakeholders, including employer groups (such as the state Chambers of Commerce and affiliates of the National Federation of Independent Business), legislators who supported and opposed duration reduction, academic experts, governor's workforce policy staff, and advocates (such as the National Employment Law Project and similar state-level organizations). We selected these states based on the magnitude of the duration reduction and the structure of the duration reductions (i.e., a mix of flat and variable maximum durations), timing of duration reduction, and geographic diversity. In the 2 duration reduction states where we were unable to interview UI officials—Florida and North Carolina—we interviewed advocates and employer groups. See table 7 for the range of stakeholders interviewed for each state.

In our interviews we asked questions about the circumstances that led to duration reduction, trust fund solvency, other recent changes to the UI program, estimates of cost savings or individuals affected, broader economic effects, and reemployment programs. We also interviewed academic experts regarding these topics, including Dr. Jeffrey Wenger, University of Georgia; Dr. Christopher J. O'Leary, W.E. Upjohn Institute for Employment Research; Dr. Patrick Conway, University of North Carolina; Dr. Michael Leachman and Dr. Chad Stone, Center on Budget and Policy Priorities; Dr. H. Luke Shaefer, University of Michigan; and Dr. Wayne Vroman, The Urban Institute. In addition, Dr. Vroman reviewed a draft of the report.

Table 7. Stakeholders Interviewed by State

State	Unemployment insurance director/staff	Governors' workforce policy advisor(s)	Employer group(s)	Legislator(s)	Academic expert(s)	Advocacy group(s)
Arkansas	✓					
Florida			✓			✓
Georgia	✓	✓	✓	✓	✓	✓
Illinois	✓					
Indiana	✓					
Kansas	✓					
Michigan	✓	✓	✓	✓	✓	✓
Missouri	✓					
North Carolina			✓		✓	✓
Ohio	✓					
South Carolina	✓					
Tennessee	✓					
Washington	✓					

Source: GAO. | GAO-15-281.

Cluster Analysis of UI and BLS Data

Additionally, we conducted a cluster analysis using data from DOL's UI program, the Bureau of Labor Statistics (BLS), and other sources. Our analysis included numerous variables, including industry composition, population over 55, unemployment rates, and trust fund loans. Cluster analysis methods assessed the degree to which these variables simultaneously were similar within various possible groups of states but were different across the groups. We used these methods to identify characteristics that were shared among states that reduced duration. Cluster analysis allowed us to identify broad, shared patterns among states across multiple variables at once, which yielded insights that can be more difficult to discern by comparing states on individual characteristics one at a time. In this way, cluster analysis can discover patterns in data, but they cannot explain why they exist or confirm causeand-effect relationships.

We used a particular form of cluster analysis, known as hierarchical agglomerative methods, to identify potential clusters of states and their decisions to reduce UI benefits. We selected variables related to program benefits and financing, as well as variables exogenous to the program, such as states' capacity to tax, selected state demographic information, and state industry composition. After collecting the variables above for all 50 states and the District of Columbia, we standardized the scales of all variables such that each variable's mean was equal to 0 and its variance was equal to 1. Because the natural scales of the variables were generally percentages, the specific method of standardization should not strongly influence our results. After standardizing the scales, we calculated a multivariate Euclidean distance matrix for all variables and states. We then applied a hierarchical agglomerative clustering algorithm to this distance matrix, which used average linkage methods to form various clusters at increasing distances.

We examined the results of the clustering algorithm to identify the individual variables that appeared to influence the results strongly. We further assessed, in concert with the political homogeneity of the state legislature and governorship, the degree to which states in various possible clusters reduced UI benefit duration. This allowed us to identify a group of benefit reduction states (Arkansas, Florida, Georgia, Missouri, North Carolina, and South Carolina) that were similar on the characteristics we analyzed, as well as benefit reduction states (Illinois, Kansas, and Michigan) that were not similar to this group. In addition, we identified comparison states (Indiana, Ohio, and Tennessee) that the algorithm clustered with the benefit reduction states but which had not reduced benefit duration. The comparison states helped us to examine why states in similar circumstances chose not to reduce benefits. For more information on the variables we examined, see table 8.

Table 8. Variables Used in Cluster Analysis

Variable	Description
Industry composition: Goods Producing	Percent of goods-producing employment (i.e., out of total non-farm employment, percent employed in construction, manufacturing, and mining and logging), to identify industry composition differences
Population 55 and over	Percent of population that is 55 or older, to identify demographic differences
Union membership	Percent of employed population who are union members
Total taxable resources: dollars per capita	A comprehensive measure of all the income flows a state can potentially tax, used by the Department of Treasury
Total taxable resources: per capita index	A per-capita index of all states' total taxable resources
Average weekly benefit amount for selected quarters	The average benefit amount paid by state UI programs

Variable	Description
Total unemployment rate	Percent of labor force that is able and available to work and is unable to find suitable work, to reflect potential claimant population
Total unemployment rate, change from previous year	Percent change in unemployment rate, to reflect economic conditions
Outstanding trust fund loan balance per covered employee	To reflect trust fund loan balance on a per-employee basis
Outstanding trust fund loan balance per covered employee, change over previous year	To reflect change in trust fund loan balance
Recipiency rate for state programs	Insured unemployed as a percent of total unemployed, to reflect participation in UI
Wage replacement ratio	Ratio that compares average weekly benefit amount to average wages, to reflect generosity of benefits
Average High Cost Multiple	The standard measure of trust fund solvency, to measure funding adequacy of UI trustfunds
Average tax rates on total wages	A 5-year average of tax on total wages as a percent, to gauge funding adequacy of UI trust funds

Source: GAO. | GAO-15-281.

Analysis of Federal and State UI Program Data

To identify the individual implications of duration reduction, we analyzed UI program data on a range of variables using data from DOL's Office of Unemployment Insurance and BLS, including the value of the foregone state and federal benefits for individuals who reach the maximum duration. We used data from DOL's Employment and Training Administration 5159 (Claims and Payment Activities) and 218 (Benefit Rights and Experience) reports, which states submit to DOL on a monthly basis. These reports include information on average weekly benefit amounts, initial claims, recipiency rates, and exhaustions. For selected variables, we analyzed data from 2006, before the recession began, to 2014, focusing on the 9 duration reduction states and the 4 states we selected that did not reduce duration. We also analyzed data from the Bureau of Labor Statistic's Current Population Survey—such as length of unemployment—and Local Area Unemployment Statistics—such as seasonally adjusted employment rates. The Current Population Survey is the nation's source of official government statistics on employment and unemployment, and it is conducted on a monthly basis with about 60,000 households. The Local Area Unemployment Statistics program provides monthly estimates of employment and unemployment for approximately 7,300 areas.

Calculation of Survival Rates

We calculated survival rates (the probability that a claimant will continue receiving benefits after a given week) based on data provided to us by Georgia and Missouri. We obtained aggregate data for each quarter on the number of claimants receiving state benefits, by benefit week, for approximately a year prior to duration reduction through two quarters following reduction. We then analyzed data from the quarter closest to each state's policy change that did not appear seasonally inflated, in order to estimate a baseline survival function prior to the policy change. Michigan provided data from a sample of claims drawn from the time period we requested. We used the estimated survival functions to estimate the possible impact of reducing maximum benefit duration in three ways. First, we calculated the probability that claimants would be affected by a maximum duration reduction, equal to the estimated survival probability at the new maximum duration. Second, we calculated the total number of claimants affected by the policy change, equal to the survival probability at the new maximum duration multiplied by the population of claimants receiving benefits at the beginning of the quarter. (We did not calculate this quantity for Michigan, due to uncertain population sizes from which our sample was drawn.) Finally, we calculated the benefit that a claimant receiving the average benefit amount in the period shortly before the policy change could have expected to lose due to a shorter maximum duration, equal to the survival probability at the new maximum duration multiplied by the total benefits received by the average recipient over the weeks exceeding the new maximum duration.

Washington State Simulation

We also asked Washington's state Employment Security Department to project the implications of reducing benefits from 26 weeks to 20 weeks, using the state's Benefit Financing Model. According to Washington officials, the model was originally developed by Wayne Vroman of the Urban Institute as part of an earlier analysis of program solvency conducted for Washington in the mid-1990's. The Washington model has continued to be used and supported by the Employment Security Department since 2000 with a review of the model completed by Dr. Vroman in June 2007,[1] and the department also conducts quarterly benchmarking on the results. The model was developed to model current law projections and legislative changes impacting Washington's trust fund account. According to Dr. Vroman, it is an actuarial model, and actuarial projections always have an element of uncertainty with the degree of uncertainty increasing as the projection extends further into the future. Macro factors such as the unemployment rate, the inflation rate and the level of statewide employment present major uncertainties.

Economic Literature Review

We also reviewed selected economic literature on key implications of UI benefits for individuals, such as labor force attachment, job search behavior, poverty reduction, and participation in other federal programs such as Social Security Disability Insurance, specifically on the effects of changing benefit levels or changing duration of eligibility for benefits. We obtained recommendations for studies from internal GAO and external UI researchers and policy experts, including DOL officials; searched various databases for peer-reviewed journal articles and other publications; and reviewed policy and research organization websites for relevant studies. Based on this research, we identified reasonable conclusions about the likely implications of duration reductions for individuals. As noted in this report, research on the questions discussed reaches different conclusions.

To identify what is known about the economic effects of reductions in benefit duration, we conducted an economic literature review that focused primarily on the stimulative effects of UI, and based on that research, we identified reasonable conclusions about the likely economic effects of duration reduction. In addition, we interviewed researchers from the Congressional Budget Office to understand its economic multiplier model. As noted in this report, research on the questions discussed reaches different conclusions. We have not done an exhaustive review of the voluminous literature on this topic.

Data Reliability

Because external data were significant to each of our research objectives, we assessed the reliability of the publicly and privately held data obtained from federal agencies and an association. To assess the reliability of DOL data sets, we administered a survey form that was specifically tailored to the system in question and addressed data uses, internal controls, and data entry practices. Once each survey was completed, we reviewed responses to assess the adequacy of the internal controls and processes in place. We determined that each data set was sufficiently reliable for the analytical purposes of this report. For data on partisan composition, we used data from the National Conference of State Legislatures. For data on total taxable resources, we obtained data from the Department of the Treasury. For these data sources beyond DOL, we obtained information on how the relevant data were generated and maintained and determined they were sufficiently reliable for the cluster analysis.

We conducted our work between November 2013 and April 2015 in accordance with generally accepted government auditing standards. Those standards require that we plan and perform the audit to obtain sufficient, appropriate evidence to provide a reasonable basis for our findings and conclusions based on our audit objectives. We believe the evidence obtained provides a reasonable basis for our findings and conclusions based on our audit objectives.

APPENDIX II: FINANCIAL CHARACTERISTICS OF SELECTED STATES

Table 9. Selected Financial Characteristics of States That Reduced Duration and States That Did Not Reduce Duration

State	Trust fund adequacy (average high cost multiple value) 2007	Trust fund loans		Capacity to tax (Total Taxable Resources, per capita index) 2010[b]
		States with a trust fund loan (2010-2012)	Average loan per covered employee[a]	
Duration Reduction States				
Arkansas	.32	✓	$295	77.5
Florida	1.04	✓	$280	90.0
Georgia	.96	✓	$194	86.8
Illinois	.34	✓	$437	107.0
Kansas	.96	✓	$0[c]	98.7
Michigan	n/a[d]	✓	$994	79.0
Missouri	.12	✓	$284	88.5
North Carolina	.23	✓	$661	92.2

State	Trust fund adequacy (average high cost multiple value) 2007	Trust fund loans: States with a trust fund loan (2010-2012)	Trust fund loans: Average loan per covered employee[a]	Capacity to tax (Total Taxable Resources, per capita index) 2010[b]
South Carolina	.26	✓	$510	76.1
Number with a trust fund loan		9		
Non-Duration Reduction States				
All states	.79[e]		$359[f]	102.1[g]
Number with a trust fund loan		27		
Selected Non-Duration Reduction States				
Indiana	.29	✓	$729	89.5
Ohio	.12	✓	$478	85.9
Tennessee	.48	✓	$0[c]	84.4
Washington	1.54		n/a	107.8
Number with a trust fund loan		3		

Source: GAO analysis of DOL data, Treasury data, and information provided by selected states. GAO-15-281.

[a] For duration reduction states, the amount shown for average loan per covered employee shown is the amount as of the fourth quarter before duration reduction became effective. For other states with loans, the amount shown is the average loan per covered employee in 2010.

[b] The total taxable resources data for 2010 are expressed as per capita, indexed values, with the per capita, indexed value for the U.S. overall set at 100.

[c] Kansas had a loan of $171 million, but repaid it before duration reduction became effective. Tennessee had a loan of about $20 million, but incurred it and repaid it within a single quarter in 2010.

[d] Because average high cost multiple (AHCM) values are derived in part from the trust fund balance, they are not calculated for states with loans. As of 2007, Michigan had already incurred a trust fund loan.

[e] This is the median AHCM value for all states that did not reduce duration.

[f] This figure represents the average loan per covered employee for the non-duration reduction states that incurred loans.

[g] This is the median total taxable resources per capita index for all states that did not reduce duration.

Table 10. Maximum Trust Fund Loan Balances, by State

State	Maximum trust fund loan balance[a] (in millions)	Month and year of maximumtrust fund loan balance[b]
Alabama	$283.0	September 2011
Arkansas	$360.0	June 2011
Arizona	$421.9	March 2012
California	$10,959.0	June 2011
Colorado	$578.2	March 2011
Connecticut	$809.9	September 2011
Delaware	$76.4	December 2012
Florida	$2,247.9	March 2011
Georgia	$752.3	March 2012
Hawaii	$49.5	March 2011
Idaho	$202.4	June 2011
Illinois	$2,951.0	March 2011
Indiana	$2,169.9	March 2011
Kansas	$170.8	September 2011
Kentucky	$958.0	March 2012
Massachusetts	$387.3	September 2010
Maryland	$133.8	September 2010
Michigan	$3,991.2	March 2011
Minnesota	$733.2	September 2011
Missouri	$861.2	March 2011
North Carolina	$2,819.9	March 2012
New Hampshire	$22.9	March 2010
New Jersey	$1,991.6	March 2011
Nevada	$823.3	March 2012
New York	$3,955.1	March 2012
Ohio	$2,611.4	June 2011
Pennsylvania	$3,761.8	June 2011
Rhode Island	$274.0	March 2012
South Carolina	$977.7	March 2011
South Dakota	$22.7	March 2010
Texas	$2,026.0	March 2010
Virginia	$467.9	March 2011
Vermont	$77.7	June 2012
Wisconsin	$1,664.8	March 2011

Source: Department of Labor. | GAO-15-281.

Notes: States that incurred and repaid a loan within the same quarter are not shown.

[a] Balances shown reflect amounts reported by states on a quarterly basis; actual trust fund loan balances may have varied on a monthly basis. For example, according to state officials, Missouri reached its actual maximum trust fund loan balance of $883 million in April 2011. Additionally, balances shown reflect principal only and do not include interest.

[b] When DOL data showed the same maximum trust fund loan balance in 2 or more successive quarters, the most recent quarter is shown.

Table 11. Federal Unemployment Tax Act (FUTA) Credit Reductions Due to States Having Outstanding Federal Advances

	Amount of tax credit reduction, by calendar year					
State	2009	2010	2011	2012	2013	2014
Arizona				0.3%		
Arkansas			0.3%	0.6%	0.9%	
California			0.3%	0.6%	0.9%	1.2%
Connecticut			0.3%	0.6%	0.9%	1.7%
Delaware				0.3%	0.6%	
Florida			0.3%	0.6%		
Georgia			0.3%	0.6%	0.9%	
Illinois			0.3%			
Indiana		0.3%	0.6%	0.9%	1.2%	1.5%
Kentucky			0.3%	0.6%	0.9%	1.2%
Michigan	0.3%	0.6%	0.9%			
Minnesota			0.3%			
Missouri			0.3%	0.6%	0.9%	
Nevada			0.3%	0.6%		
New Jersey			0.3%	0.6%		
New York			0.3%	0.6%	0.9%	1.2%
North Carolina			0.3%	0.6%	0.9%	1.2%
Ohio			0.3%	0.6%	0.9%	1.2%
Pennsylvania			0.3%			
Rhode Island			0.3%	0.6%	0.9%	
South Carolina		0.3%	[a]	[a]	[a]	
Vermont				0.3%		
Virginia			0.3%			
Wisconsin			0.3%	0.6%	0.9%	

Source: Department of Labor. | GAO-15-281.

[a] According to DOL, South Carolina qualified for avoidance of its FUTA tax credit reduction. See 26 U.S.C. § 3302(g).

Appendix III: Specifications for Variable Maximum Durations, Estimated Cost Savings, and Additional UI Program Changes for Selected States

Table 12. State Specifications for Variable Maximum Durations of Unemployment Insurance Benefits

		Description of variable maximum duration			
State	*Variable maximum duration (weeks)*	*Maximum duration available (weeks)*[a]	*Corresponding state unemployment rate*	*Maximum duration following duration reduction (weeks)*	*Maximum durationas of October2014 (weeks)*
Florida	12-23	12	5 percent or less	23[b]	16[b]
		13-22	Each .5 percent increase in the unemployment rate above 5 percent triggers an additional week		
		23	10.5 percent or more		
Georgia	14-20	14	6.5 percent or less	19	15
		15-19	Each .5 percent increase in the unemployment rate triggers an additional week		
		20	9 percent or more		
Kansas	16-26	16	Less than 4.5 percent	20	20
		20	4.5 percent to less than 6 percent		
		26	6 percent or more		
North Carolina	12-20	12	5.5 percent or less	19[b]	14[b]
		13-19	Each .5 percent increase in the unemployment rate triggers an additional week		
		20	More than 9 percent		

Source: Applicable state laws and information provided by state UI officials. | GAO-15-281.

[a] Duration is determined annually or semi-annually, depending on state law, in accordance with the state's total unemployment rate.

[b] Florida and North Carolina did not provide information about the maximum durations that were in effect following duration reduction or as of October 2014. We imputed these durations based on the applicable unemployment rates, as calculated by BLS.

Table 13. Estimated Cost Savings Attributable to Duration Reduction and Maximum Loan Balances in Selected States

State	Year duration reduction enacted	Amount of reduction (weeks)	Estimated cumulative cost savings since duration reduction(millions)[a]	Maximum trust fund loan balance (millions)[b]	Cumulative cost savingsas a percent of maximumtrust fund loan balance
Arkansas	2011	1	$16.7	$360	4.6
Illinois	2011[c]	1	$100	$2,951	3.4
Michigan	2011	6	$391	$3,991	9.8
Missouri	2011	6	$387	$861	44.9

Source: GAO analysis of relevant state laws and information provided by states and the Department of Labor. | GAO-15-281.

Notes: The maximum trust fund loan represents only the amount owed to the federal government, not the amount needed in each state to replenish the trust fund. States set their own targets for their trust funds. For example, Georgia's target is $1 billion and Michigan's is $2.5 billion.

[a] State officials in Illinois and Michigan provided cumulative cost savings estimates in October 2014; Michigan's estimate covers the period from January 15, 2012 to June 30, 2014. Totals for the other states were calculated by GAO. In Arkansas, officials estimated that duration reduction represented a savings of $5 million each year. Missouri officials estimated a cost savings of $108 million each year.

[b] The maximum trust fund balances shown are based on quarterly data. Arkansas' trust fund loan balance reached its maximum in the quarter ending in June 2011; Illinois', in March 2011; Michigan's, in March 2011; and Missouri's, in March 2011. However, a state's actual balance may have varied in a given month. For example, according to state officials, Missouri reached its maximum trust fund loan balance of $883 million in April 2011. Based on this balance, the cost savings for Missouri represent 43.8 percent of the maximum trust fund loan balance.

[c] Illinois' duration reduction was only applicable to claims filed in 2012.

Table 14. Additional Financing and Benefit Changes Made by Duration Reduction States

	Increases in employer taxes					Changes to eligibility			
State	Taxable wage base	Tax rates	Surtaxes	Bond issue	Reduced average weekly benefit amount	Monetary	Non-monetary	Program integrity changes	Changes to application procedures
Arkansas	✓	✓				✓	✓	✓	
Florida						✓	✓	✓	✓
Georgia	✓	✓	✓[a]				✓[c]	✓	✓
Illinois	✓[a]		✓[a]	✓				✓	
Kansas	✓					✓	✓	✓	
Michigan	✓[a]			✓[b]			✓[c]	✓	
Missouri							✓[d]	✓	
North Carolina		✓			✓[e]		✓	✓	
South Carolina	✓	✓[a]	✓[a]			✓	✓[d]	✓	✓

Source: GAO analysis of information provided by states, the Department of Labor, and GAO review of relevant state laws in selected states, generally confirmed by state officials. Because UI officials in Florida and North Carolina did not respond to our questions, we were unable to confirm the information for these states with state officials. The table generally reflects any relevant changes states reported making around the time of duration reduction through October 2014, although for Florida, Kansas, and North Carolina, the table only reflects changes made by the specific piece of legislation that reduced duration. I GAO-15-281

[a] State officials described these changes as temporary. In some cases, automatic readjustments may be tied to the condition of the trust fund balance. For example, according to state officials, in Michigan, if the trust fund reaches $2.5 billion for 2 consecutive quarters, the taxable wage base will revert from $9,500 to its previous level of $9,000.

[b] Michigan issued bonds in the amount of $3.3 billion to repay its loan. Although employers must pay a special assessment to repay the bond, the interest rate was more favorable to the state than the federal loan would have been, according to state officials. Additionally, officials state that, by repaying the federal loan in this way, the state avoided FUTA tax credit reductions for its employers.

[c] These states reported changes to work search requirements among the non-monetary eligibility changes. In addition, Michigan reported revising the definition of "suitable work" to include positions outside the claimant's experience as long as they pay a common or prevalent wage or meet other criteria, and providing for disqualification for chronic absenteeism or negligent loss of credentials, such as a commercial driver's license.

[d] These states reported changes to the definition of misconduct among the non-monetary eligibility changes.

[e] In February 2013, North Carolina enacted legislation that reduced benefit amounts as of July 2013, thereby losing eligibility for the emergency benefits program,

according to CRS. However, states that made changes to their benefit amounts before March 1, 2012 are not subject to the nonreduction requirement. Pub. L. No. 112-96, § 2144, 126 Stat. 156, 171 (2012).

APPENDIX IV: WASHINGTON STATE SIMULATION USING BENEFIT FINANCING MODEL

We asked Washington State's UI agency, the Employment Security Department, to project the implications of reducing benefits from 26 weeks to 20 weeks, using the state's Benefit Financing Model. The model was originally developed by Wayne Vroman of the Urban Institute as part of an earlier analysis of program solvency conducted for Washington in the mid-1990s. According to state officials, the Washington model has continued to be used and supported by the state since 2000 with a review of the model completed by Dr. Vroman in June 2007,[1] and the state also conducts quarterly benchmarking on the results. The model was developed to model current law projections and legislative changes impacting the UI trust fund account.

Table 16 below shows the impact of a reduced maximum duration on key UI benefit variables in 2013 under two scenarios. The first scenario reflects current law assumptions while the proposal shows the same benefit variables assuming a 20 weeks maximum duration. Assuming a reduction in the maximum duration from 26 weeks to 20 weeks would have led to a 9.5 percent reduction in total benefit payments in 2013.

Table 15. Impact of Benefit Reduction on Washington State 2013 Benefits

	2013	
UI Variable	Current law (maximum duration of 26 weeks)	Alternative scenario (maximum duration of 20 weeks)
Weeks compensated	3,162,052	2,861,657
First payments	195,029	195,029
Exhaustions	70.084	105,323
Exhaustion rate	35.7%	52.2%
Survival rate	96.0%	96.6%
Actual duration	16.3	14.7
Average weekly benefit amount	$389.00	$389.00
Total benefits paid	$1,230,038,228	$1,113,184,596

Source: GAO analysis of Washington State Employment Security Department data. I GAO-15-281.

According to state officials, Washington has a system with two taxes. The first tax is experience-based and indexed to the benefit ratio. The other is a "social tax" that is assessed yearly and is mandated by statute to collect the amount required to make sure the UI trust fund remains solvent.

The state UI agency applied the 9.5 percent reduction in weeks compensated that was calculated in 2013 to the UI model starting in 2015. As a result, UI tax collections would be reduced by $381 million from 2016 through 2020 and tax rates in all years from 2016 forward would also be decreased. The Employment Security Department estimated that by 2020, duration reduction would increase the UI trust fund balance by $257 million.

APPENDIX V: ANALYSIS OF INDIVIDUAL STATES

Table 16. Highest Tier of Emergency Compensation Benefits Available in Duration Reduction States, 2008-2013

State	Highest Tier	Tier at Effective Date ofDuration Reduction
Arkansas	Tier III	Tier III
Florida	Tier IV	Tier IV
Georgia	Tier IV	Tier IV
Illinois	Tier IV	Tier IV
Kansas	Tier III	None
Michigan	Tier IV	Tier III
Missouri	Tier IV	Tier IV
North Carolina	Tier IV	Tier I
South Carolina	Tier IV	Tier IV

Source: GAO analysis of DOL data. I GAO-15-281

Note: When 20 weeks of extended benefits are available, claimants could have received up to following maximum total weeks: Tier I, 66 weeks; Tier II, 80 weeks; Tier III, 93 weeks; Tier IV, 99 weeks.

Table 17. Effective Dates of Extended Benefits for Reduction States, 2008-2013

State	Effective Dates of Extended Benefits (weeks ending)
Arkansas	April 18, 2009 to September 26, 2009
Florida	February 28, 2009 to January 2, 2010 May 29, 2010 to May 12, 2012
Georgia	February 28, 2009 to April 21, 2012

State	Effective Dates of Extended Benefits (weeks ending)
Illinois	April 11, 2009 to June 27, 2009 July 11, 2009 to May 12, 2012
Kansas	July 11, 2009 to April 7, 2012
Michigan	January 31, 2009 to February 18, 2012
Missouri	June 20, 2009 to April 7, 2012
North Carolina	January 3, 2009 to May 12, 2012
South Carolina	March 14, 2009 to April 7, 2012

Source: GAO analysis of DOL data. I GAO-15-281.

We examined economic and UI program data from DOL to see whether we could discern any implications the duration reductions may have had for individuals. We identified key indicators that describe unemployed persons in reduction states in comparison with nonreduction states and with the United States overall, according to our analysis of selected data.[1] We found that individuals in states that reduced benefit duration were more likely to be unemployed for a longer period of time but were less likely to be using UI than individuals in other states, particularly after duration reductions. Table 18 shows the data we analyzed and differences between reduction and non-reduction states, if any.

Table 18. GAO Analysis of Selected 2006-2014 Data and Results

Data	Nationwide trends	Duration reduction state trends
Length of unemployment	From 2008 to 2011, the average length of unemployment increased in all duration reduction states and nonreduction states overall.	Length of unemployment for all those unemployed decreased after duration reduction in these states. Duration reduction states generally had longer averagelengths of unemployment than nonreduction states.
Labor force participation (people working or available to work)	Labor force participation has declined at a steady rate across the United States since 2006, even as the economy improved following the recent recession.	Labor force participation declined following duration reduction in most of these states.

Table 18. (Continued)

Data	Nationwide trends	Duration reduction state trends
Unemployment rate	Unemployment has declined at a steady rate across the United States since the beginning of 2010.	Unemployment rates declined following duration reduction in most of these states. Duration reduction states, on average, had higher unemployment rates than nonreduction states, particularly in 2009.
Exhaustion of UI benefits	Exhaustion rates increased during the recession, but have declined across the United States since 2010.	Duration reduction states, on average, had higher exhaustion rates than non-reduction states before, during, and after the recession. In some states exhaustion rates increased after reduction, but in other states, rates decreased.
Average duration on unemployment benefits	Average duration spiked at the beginning of 2010, but has declined across the United States since then, and remained relatively flat since the end of 2011.	Average duration on unemployment benefits declined in most duration reduction states after 2010. Generally, duration reduction states have lower average durations than nonreduction states. In some states, average duration declined after reduction, but ina few states it rose.
Participation in UI (recipiency rates, or the percentage of people unemployed who are collecting unemployment benefits that week)	Recipiency rates have generally declined since 2009, with the exception of seasonal spikes.	Duration reduction states generally have lower recipiency rates than the average of nonreduction states. This difference increased toward the end of the time period we analyzed.

Source: GAO analysis of DOL data. I GAO-15-28.

Dynamics of the Larger Economy

Although these distinctions exist, it is not possible to attribute them to the duration reductions without controlling for the greater economic context and other factors. For example, many of the other factors that likely had an effect include the dynamics of the larger economy, availability of federal UI benefits, and other changes made to state UI programs during the same period.

Dynamics of the Larger Economy

The economic recovery following the recession affected trends such as average duration on UI and average length of unemployment.[2] The national unemployment rate decreased from a high of 10 percent in October 2009 to 5.6 percent in September 2014. In addition, the magnitude of the recession in terms of the substantial numbers of private-sector jobs lost, and more modest gains in jobs during the recovery, had an impact on the trends we analyzed (see fig. 11).

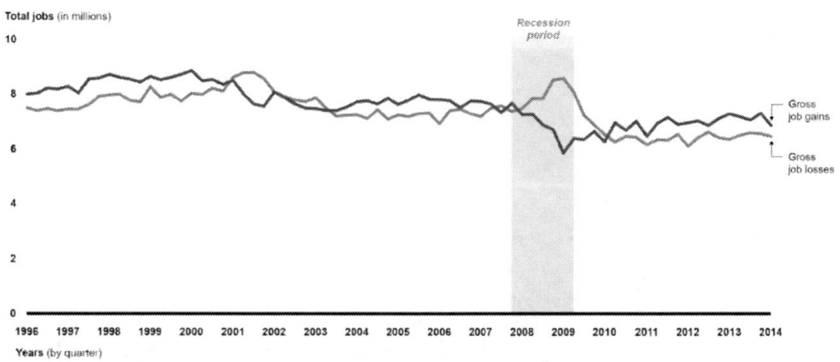

Source: GAO analysis of US ureau of Labor Statistics data. | GAO-15-281.

Figure 11. Annual Private-Sector Gross Job Gains and Losses, 1994-2014.

Furthermore, despite the decline in the unemployment rate, the participation rate for the civilian labor force continues to decline to historically low levels, reflecting departures from the labor force altogether.[3]

Availability of Federal Benefits

The effects of the changes in state UI benefit durations were mitigated by the duration of federal benefits, which were largely available when state duration reductions went into effect. For example, the total number of weeks available, including federal benefits, reached 46, 53, and 99 weeks at different points in time in various states, according to the Congressional Research Service. The availability of these federal benefits would affect any impact of duration reductions.

Other UI Program Changes

UI program changes, such as restrictions on eligibility, could also have affected participation in the UI program. For example, according to state officials, South Carolina's new definition of "gross misconduct" now results in immediate, full disqualification for any claimant engaging in certain behaviors, such as illegal drug use during either work or non-work hours. Other states, including Georgia, implemented stronger work search requirements, according to their UI directors. Florida mandated that applications only be done online and that applicants complete a skill assessment intended to help develop a reemployment plan, which, according to advocates with whom we spoke, could deter some individuals from completing their applications.

End Notes

[1] During the recovery following the recent recession, the federal government provided UI benefits through two major programs, Emergency Unemployment Compensation and Extended Benefits, which we refer to as "federal programs" and "federal benefits" in this report. The federal government funded benefits under Emergency Unemployment Compensation. Under federal law, benefits in the Extended Benefits program are generally funded by both the federal government and the states; however, under the American Recovery and Reinvestment Act of 2009 as amended, the federal government fully funded these benefits through December 31, 2013. Throughout this report, we use "state program" and "state benefits" to refer to the initial period of state-provided UI benefits that most states provide for up to 26 weeks.

[2] We also asked state officials to confirm our understanding of state laws. Among the 9 states that reduced duration, officials from 2—Florida and North Carolina— did not respond to our written questions. We interviewed advocates and employer groups in both of these states.

[3] For the purposes of this report, the District of Columbia is treated as a state. While Puerto Rico and the Virgin Islands also participate in the UI program, they are not included in the scope of this report.

[4] In addition to DOL and selected states, other sources included the Department of the Treasury and the National Conference of State Legislatures for selected variables.

[5] See Background Material and Data on Programs within the Jurisdiction of the Committee on Ways and Means (Green Book) (Washington, D.C.: November 2014).

[6] Although there are no federal requirements for the minimum or maximum time states must provide benefits, in a 1996 report to the President and the Congress, an advisory body composed of labor and employer representatives, state officials, and a researcher

recommended a duration of 6 months—i.e., 26 weeks. See Advisory Council on Unemployment Compensation, Collected Findings and Recommendations 1994-1996 (Washington, D.C.: 1996).

[7] Daniel N. Price, Unemployment Insurance, Then and Now, 1935-1985 (Social Security Bulletin, vol. 48, no. 10, October 1985).

[8] Currently, according to DOL, two states provide benefits for longer than 26 weeks: Montana provides 28 weeks and Massachusetts provides 30 weeks.

[9] There is some evidence of reduction in the duration of state benefits that predated the current duration reductions. Specifically, in 1993, we reviewed UI program changes in 7 states, and found that 2 of them—Massachusetts and New Hampshire—had reduced duration, in concert with other changes. In Massachusetts' case, we found that the reduction was from 30 weeks to 26 weeks. According to DOL, as of January 2015, maximum duration in Massachusetts is 30 weeks. See GAO, Unemployment Insurance: Program's Ability to Meet Objectives Jeopardized, GAO/HRD-93-107 (Washington, D.C.: September 28, 1993). However, according to an outside expert who reviewed a draft of this report, the scale of the current duration reductions is unprecedented.

[10] None of the officials from the 7 duration reduction states where we were able to conduct interviews identified any successful efforts in their states to restore duration to 26 weeks.

[11] This discussion of state eligibility requirements is based on DOL's Comparison of State Unemployment Insurance Laws, 2014 (Washington, D.C.: 2015).

[12] According to DOL, most states calculate the durations that claimants are eligible for based on their earnings or employment history. That is, they determine the maximum benefit an individual may receive, either by calculating the amount as a fraction or percent of wages earned during a specified period, or they set maximum weeks of benefits as a fraction of weeks worked during a specified period and then divide the maximum benefit by the state's average weekly benefit amount to determine weeks of benefits. These methods can result in durations for individual claimants that are less that the state's maximum. By contrast, as of January 1, 2014, 8 states did not use either of these methods, and provided benefits for 26 weeks for all claimants. See DOL, Comparison of State Unemployment Insurance Laws, 2014 (Washington, D.C.: 2015).

[13] According to DOL, those who voluntarily leave their jobs are generally ineligible for UI. However, some states allow exceptions, such as accepting a layoff to avoid bumping another worker, leaving employment after being directed to perform an illegal act, or leaving employment due to unsafe working conditions. States also vary in their definitions of "misconduct," which generally refers to intentional and substantial disregard of the employer's interests, and in the applicable penalties for misconduct. States provide for heavier penalties in cases of dishonesty or criminal acts, but in some cases, misconduct can result in temporary suspension of benefits, depending on state law. See DOL, Comparison of State Unemployment Insurance Laws, 2014.

[14] Pub. L. No. 110-252, Title IV, 122 Stat. 2353, 2353.

[15] Katelin P. Isaacs and Julie M. Whittaker, Emergency Unemployment Compensation (EUC08): Status of Benefits Prior to Expiration, R42444 (Washington, D.C.: Congressional Research Service, August 11, 2014).

[16] North Carolina made other changes to its UI program that made it ineligible to receive emergency benefits as of June 29, 2013, according to CRS.

[17] The extended benefits program comes into effect and pays unemployment benefits when a state's unemployment rate is increasing and reaches certain levels. All states must pay up to 13 weeks of extended benefits if the unemployment rate among those eligible for UI for a

specified 13-week period is at least 5 percent and is 120 percent of the average of the rates for the same 13-week period in each of the two previous years. States can also choose to pay an additional 7 weeks of extended benefits if the unemployment rate among those eligible reaches certain thresholds and is increasing.

[18] This period exceeded the maximum total duration of 72 weeks available in some states during the recession of 2002-2004, which duration reflected another temporary UI program created at the time, the Temporary Extension of Unemployment Compensation. See Henry S. Farber and Robert G. Valletta, Do Extended Unemployment Benefits Lengthen Unemployment Spells? Evidence From Recent Cycles In The U.S. Labor Market, Working Paper 19048 (Cambridge, Massachusetts: National Bureau of Economic Research, May 2013).

[19] The most recent emergency benefits program provided potentially four tiers, or levels, of benefits. Under the most recent rules for this program, the first two tiers provided up to 54 percent of state benefit duration, the third tier provided up to 35 percent of state benefit duration, and the fourth tier provided up to 39 percent of state benefit duration. Under sequestration, which applies to emergency benefits, as well as to the federal share of extended benefits, to assist states in their efforts to comply with the cuts required by sequestration, DOL has allowed states to make changes to the administration of emergency benefits, including changes to duration of benefits. See Julie M. Whittaker and Katelin P. Isaacs, Unemployment Insurance: Programs and Benefits RL33362 (Washington, D.C.: Congressional Research Service, February 12, 2014).

[20] The term "forward funding" usually refers to budget authority that is made available for obligation beginning in the last quarter of the fiscal year for the financing of ongoing activities (usually grant programs) during the next fiscal year. GAO, A Glossary of Terms Used in the Federal Budget Process, GAO-05-734SP (September 2005). However, in this report we use "forward funding" to refer to the practice of states accumulating reserves in unemployment insurance trust funds in anticipation of increased outlays in the future.

[21] Federal trust funds link designated monies with a specific purpose or program. They are included in the unified budget, which provides information on the federal government's overall fiscal policy—the aggregate size of the government and its borrowing requirements. See GAO, Federal Trust and Other Earmarked Funds: Answers to Frequently Asked Questions, GAO-01-199SP (Washington, D.C.: January 1, 2001).

[22] This discussion of state tax provisions is based on DOL's Comparison of State Unemployment Insurance Laws, 2014 (Washington, D.C.: 2015) and UWC— Strategic Services on Unemployment & Workers' Compensation, Highlights of State Unemployment Compensation Laws 2014. Although these taxes are paid by the employer, economists generally have concluded that their cost is likely to be borne by workers. Additionally, 3 states—Alaska, Pennsylvania, and New Jersey—directly levy UI taxes on workers.

[23] In 2014, states' taxable wage bases ranged from $7,000 in Arizona to $41,300 in Washington. UWC—Strategic Services on Unemployment & Workers' Compensation, Highlights of State Unemployment Compensation Laws 2014.

[24] In 2014, the lowest minimum tax rate for employers was 0 percent in Iowa, Missouri, Nebraska, and South Dakota, and the highest maximum tax rate was12.9 percent in Arkansas. UWC—Strategic Services on Unemployment & Workers' Compensation, Highlights of State Unemployment Compensation Laws 2014.

[25] However, a federal "nonreduction" rule made the availability of federally financed emergency benefits conditional on a state not actively changing its method of calculating UI benefits, if doing so would decrease weekly benefit amounts. Automatic adjustments to weekly benefit

amounts that exist in some states do not violate the nonreduction rule. The American Recovery and Reinvestment Act of 2009 also temporarily provided an additional $25 weekly benefit per claimant. This benefit was known as Federal Additional Compensation (FAC). One condition (known as the "nonreduction rule") for states to be eligible for FAC was that the state could not modify the method for calculating regular UI benefits such that the average weekly benefit amounts would decrease from their levels in place December 31, 2008. Although this benefit expired in 2010, soon thereafter, the nonreduction rule was attached to the emergency benefits program.

[26] Specifically, if a state has an outstanding loan balance on January 1 for two consecutive years, the full amount of the loan must be repaid by November 10 of the second year, or employers in that state lose 0.3 percent of the FUTA tax credit. For example, we previously reported that, if a state borrows to pay UI benefits and has an outstanding loan balance on the second subsequent January 1, the FUTA tax credit is reduced, and in such instances, according to DOL, employers' effective FUTA rate jumps from 0.6 percent to .9 percent. Federal law also sets forth formulas for determining the amount of the reduction in states with loan balances outstanding for 3 or more years. 26 U.S.C. § 3302. According to DOL, each 0.3 percent reduction in the tax credit represents up to $21 in additional employer taxes per worker per year, on the current $7,000 taxable wage base. Additionally, such tax credit reductions affect employers in a state, without regard to their experience rating. For more information, see Appendix II.

[27] Some states may choose to repay federal trust fund loans by securing loans in the private bond market. By doing so, states can use the proceeds from private loans to repay borrowing from the federal government, and then levy higher payroll taxes on employers to repay the private loans. Although the state remains in debt, the state may be able to negotiate a lower interest rate and, because the federal government has been repaid, avoids FUTA tax credit reductions.

[28] Gay Gilbert, National Unemployment Insurance Program Update, U.S. Department of Labor, Employment and Training Administration, June 18, 2014.

[29] Reserve ratios are UI trust fund levels as a percentage of total annual statewide wages.

[30] The high cost multiple is derived by dividing the reserve ratio by the high cost rate, which is the highest historical ratio of benefits to wages for a 12-month period in a particular state.

[31] The average high cost rate is the average of the three highest calendar year benefit cost rates in the last 20 years or the period covering the last 3 recessions, if longer.

[32] See Advisory Council on Unemployment Compensation, Collected Findings and Recommendations 1994-1996 (Washington, D.C.: 1996), and 20 C.F.R. § 606.32. Beginning in 2019, DOL's regulations on interest relief implement an AHCM solvency criterion of 1.00, for purposes of rounding.

[33] See GAO, Unemployment Insurance Trust Funds: Long-standing State Financing Policies Have Increased Risk of Insolvency, GAO-10-440 (Washington, D.C.: April 14, 2010).

[34] Of these six characteristics, we identified five through a technique known as cluster analysis. Other characteristics that we considered—state industry composition, state population age 55 and over, and UI program variables such as recipiency rate and exhaustion rate—less clearly distinguished duration reduction states from states that did not reduce duration. See appendix I for a list of all characteristics reviewed. The sixth characteristic that distinguished states that reduced duration from those that did not— political homogeneity— was analyzed separately. For a description of other characteristics of duration reduction states, such as the status of Medicaid expansion, tax system progressivity, and the labor force and long-term unemployed population by race and ethnicity, see Josh Bivens, Joshua

Smith, and Valerie Wilson, State Cuts to Jobless Benefits Did Not Help Workers or Taxpayers (Economic Policy Institute, Briefing Paper 380, July 28, 2014).

[35] Among the 42 states that did not reduce duration, in the fourth quarter of 2007, AHCM values ranged from .09 in New York to 1.88 in Hawaii.

[36] Officials in 2 of the 9 duration reduction states—Florida and North Carolina—declined to respond to our question about the rationale for duration reduction. Among the states whose UI officials discussed the rationale for duration reduction, officials in 5 states cautioned that they had little or no direct knowledge of their legislatures' rationale for duration reduction.

[37] Because state tax rates vary widely, and include both maximum and minimum tax rates, we analyzed the average tax rate on total wages—total employer contributions for a 12- month period divided by the total wages paid by taxable employers for the same period. We analyzed quarterly data for a 5-year period—2006 to 2010—before duration reductions were adopted in any state. The U.S. average for this period was .69 percent, and 3 of the 6 states that reduced duration in 2011 had tax rates below this level. Of the 3 states that reduced duration after 2011, 2 had average tax rates below the U.S. average for the 5 years before they reduced duration. However, this variable was not among the characteristics that most distinguished the states that reduced duration from those that did not. For more information, see appendix I.

[38] These stakeholders were labor advocates in all 4 states as well as employer groups in 3 states. The 4 states were Florida, Georgia, Michigan, and North Carolina. In 2 of these states, employer groups noted that such actions had contributed to the weakness of their states' trust fund balances.

[39] See GAO-10-440.

[40] Under federal law, the Department of the Treasury is required to produce annual estimates of Total Taxable Resources (TTR), Treasury's estimates of the relative fiscal capacity of the states. See 42 U.S.C. § 300x-7. TTR is a flow concept, and is the unduplicated sum of the income flows produced within a state and the income flows received by its residents that a state can potentially tax. TTR does not consider the actual fiscal choices made by states. It measures all income flows a state can potentially tax.

[41] In 2010, the median TTR indexed per capita value for the duration reduction states was 88.5, and the median for states that did not reduce duration was 102.4. South Carolina, Arkansas, and Michigan had TTR values that ranged from 76.1 to 79.0, among the seven lowest TTR indexed per capita values in the country. The TTR indexed per capita values for all 9 duration reduction states ranged from 76.1 to 107.0; by contrast, the values for the states that did not reduce duration ranged from 71.1 to 194.4.

[42] For the duration reduction states, we measured the unemployment rate in the quarter preceding the enactment of duration reduction for each state.

[43] Of the 8 states that had state legislatures and governorships aligned with a single party when duration reductions were enacted, 6 (Florida, Georgia, Kansas, Michigan, North Carolina, and South Carolina) were aligned with the Republican Party and 2 (Arkansas and Illinois) were aligned with the Democratic Party. Missouri had divided government at the time.

[44] See Pub. L. No. 110-252, § 4001(g), 122 Stat. 2323, 2353, as amended, codified at 26 U.S.C. § 3304 note. While officials in 4 of the 7 states where we conducted interviews did identify the nonreduction requirement as a possible factor, officials in 2 states said it was not a consideration, and officials in 1 of these 2 states said that duration reduction was adopted before it took effect. In the remaining state, UI officials indicated they did not know if it was a consideration.

[45] States set their own targets for trust fund levels. For example, Georgia's target for its trust fund is $1 billion and Michigan's is $2.5 billion, according to state officials.

[46] Of the 9 duration reduction states, 2 did not respond to our written questions.

[47] Employer groups consistently told us that they supported duration reduction and considered the employer tax increases as necessary to restore solvency. Although concerned about their tax burden, employers generally characterized the tax increases as preferable to the status quo, which appeared "unsustainable" to them because they faced additional burdens, such as automatic tax increases to repay the federal loan, future FUTA tax credit reductions if their states' loans were not repaid in a timely way, and greater burdens under the state's system for increasing an employer's tax rates according to its layoff records.

[48] These cost savings estimates are subject to limitations, such as their basis in economic conditions that may have changed. The states that provided estimates included 2 with 1-week reductions and 2 with 6-week reductions. It is possible that states with larger reductions realized greater cost savings. However, an analysis of North Carolina's adoption of a larger reduction—down to a variable duration of 12-20 weeks—found that it contributed less to program solvency than that state's reduction in benefit amounts. See Alexandra Forter Sirota, What's the Harm? Plenty: Unemployment Insurance Changes Threaten the State's Economy and Hurt the Unemployed (North Carolina Justice Center, BTC Reports, vol. 20, no. 5, July 2014).

[49] According to the Department of Labor, 8 states issued bonds to repay their trust fund loans: Arizona, Colorado, Idaho, Illinois, Michigan, Nevada, Pennsylvania, and Texas.

[50] In February 2013, North Carolina enacted legislation that reduced benefit amounts as of July 2013, thereby losing eligibility for the emergency benefits program, according to CRS. However, states that made changes to their benefit amounts before March 1, 2012 are not subject to the nonreduction requirement. Pub. L. No. 112-96, § 2144, 126 Stat. 156, 171 (2012). Historically, following recessions, states have made changes to areas such as employer taxes, eligibility, and benefits. For example, in a review of changes by 7 states between 1978 and 1992, we found that all had increased employer taxes, and some strengthened disqualification provisions, increased the taxable wage base, and decreased the minimum benefit amount. Two of the states reduced duration. See GAO, Unemployment Insurance: Program's Ability to Meet Objectives Jeopardized, GAO/HRD-93-107 (Washington, D.C.: Sept. 28, 1993).

[51] The American Recovery and Reinvestment Act of 2009 had offered incentives to states to expand eligibility in certain ways. See Pub. L. No. 111-5, § 2003, 123 Stat. 115, 439. Eligibility restrictions have the effect of limiting the size of the population drawing claims.

[52] Furthermore, in 2 of the 4 states where we spoke with employers, employer groups noted that program integrity efforts helped build support for other changes, which included tax increases. Program integrity initiatives, similar to eligibility restrictions, can limit the size of the population drawing claims.

[53] In addition to their loans, these states were selected based on their similarity to the duration reduction states according to criteria including weaker trust funds, lower overall ability to tax, and state unemployment rate. See appendix I.

[54] Ohio UI officials noted that state law requires annual adjustment of monetary eligibility requirements and benefits, but makes no similar provision for changes in employer taxes.

[55] According to information provided by an official in one comparison state, eligibility changes were enacted to reverse previous expansions of eligibility under federal law, such as eligibility based on part-time employment.

[56] In addition to being similar in terms of the condition of their trust fund balances before the recession, 2 of these 3 states had high loan amounts per employee, and all 3 had low total taxable resources, high unemployment rates, and political homogeneity (see app. I). In 2010, all 3 states had divided governments, but all had Republican-led legislatures and governors in 2011, 2012, and 2013. While the comparison state that did not have a federal trust fund loan—Washington—was unlike these states and unlike the duration reduction states in some respects, such as having an adequate trust fund balance before the recession, it did have political homogeneity, since it had a Democratic-led legislature and governor in every year from 2010 to 2013.

[57] However, we asked officials in Washington to model the effects of a reduction from 26 to 20 weeks on the state's trust fund and on employer taxes. For more information, see appendix IV.

[58] One researcher has found a trend toward longer spells of unemployment, based on analysis of data over two decades. See Wayne Vroman, Low Benefit Recipiency in State Unemployment Insurance Programs, Urban Institute, June 2001.

[59] Federal extended benefits were available in some states during 2008, and were jointly financed by the state and federal governments until early 2009, when they were temporarily fully funded by the federal government through 2013.

[60] In order to estimate the affected population in each state, we requested data on the population receiving benefits up to 26 weeks before and after the implementation of duration reduction from selected duration reduction states (for example, we excluded Illinois, where the reduction applied to claims filed in 2012). Based on data provided by 2 states, we estimated that duration reduction would have affected about 20,600 claimants in Missouri in the fourth quarter of 2010 and about 19,000 claimants in Georgia in the second quarter of 2012, assuming an 18-week maximum duration. States do collect data on benefits received after 26 weeks.

[61] While the phenomenon of state reduction to benefit periods is generally very recent, existing research on differences in benefit amounts and durations caused by federal UI program supplements may inform the question of their impact on individual UI claimants.

[62] See, for example, Katharine Bradbury, Labor Market Transitions and the Availability of Unemployment Insurance (Federal Reserve Bank of Boston, Working Paper No. 14-2, July 9, 2014).

[63] David Grubb, Assessing the Impact of Recent Unemployment Insurance Extensions in the United States, Working Paper (Paris: Organization for Economic Cooperation and Development, May 2011).

[64] In addition, other implications for individuals of unemployment have been addressed in the literature. For example, unemployed workers face depletion of savings, or the need to use credit cards to meet household expenses. In addition, there are implications for physical and mental health, and other variables. (See, for example, Cliff Zukin, Dr. Carl E. Van Horn, and Charley Stone, Categorizing the Unemployed by the Impact of the Recession, Working Paper (John J. Heldrich Center for Workforce Development, December 2011) and Kaiser Family Foundation/NPR, Long-Term Unemployed Survey (December 2011). Because these implications relate more to the condition of being unemployed than to the receipt of UI per se, and because it is difficult to determine how, if at all, they are affected by shorter durations of UI benefits, this report does not address these issues.

[65] Carmen DeNavas-Walt and Bernadette D. Proctor, Income and Poverty in the United States: 2013, (U.S. Census Bureau Current Population Reports, September 2014).

[66] Robert A. Moffitt, Unemployment benefits and unemployment, (IZA World of Labor, May 2014).

[67] GAO, Unemployment Insurance: Economic Circumstances of Individuals Who Exhausted Benefits, GAO-12-408, (Washington, D.C.: February 17, 2012).

[68] Report by the U.S. Congress Joint Economic Committee, Does Unemployment Insurance Inhibit Job Search? Report by the U.S. Congress Joint Economic Committee (July 2010).

[69] Andreas I. Mueller, Jesse Rothstein, and Till M. von Wachter, Unemployment Insurance and Disability Insurance in the Great Recession, Working Paper 19672 (National Bureau of Economic Research, November 2013).

[70] This assumes 47 weeks of emergency unemployment compensation and the higher level of extended benefits are in effect in both scenarios. According to the Congressional Research Service, from November 8, 2009, to September 1, 2012, as much as 99 weeks of benefits was available; however, from September 2012-December 2013, 93 weeks was the maximum available.

[71] While all 9 duration reduction states participated in the federal extended and emergency benefit programs, they varied in the timing of their reductions and therefore the length of available federal benefits at the time of the reduction (see app. V for more information on the federal benefit programs and the duration reduction states).

[72] For both Missouri and Georgia, we used data on the number of claimants who collected a particular week of benefits during the calendar year quarter before duration reduction. For example, in Missouri, 19,290 people collected week 21 of benefits during the first quarter of 2011.

[73] This analysis assumes no changes in individual behavior, such as finding employment faster due to the reduction in state benefits. In the presence of federal benefits, one would not expect such behavioral changes as the claimant still receives benefits regardless of the source.

[74] As previously mentioned, we analyzed data on benefits up to 26 weeks, in part to estimate the affected population. States do collect data on benefits after the 26th week.

[75] GAO, State and Local Governments: Knowledge of Past Recessions Can Inform Future Federal Fiscal Assistance, GAO-11-401 (Washington, D.C.: March 31, 2011).

[76] GAO, GAO Cost Estimating and Assessment Guide: Best Practices for Developing and Managing Capital Program Costs, GAO 09-3SP (Washington, D.C.: March 2009).

[77] Katelin P. Isaacs, Unemployment Insurance: Consequences of Changes in State Unemployment Compensation Laws, R41859 (Washington, D.C.: Congressional Research Service, August 19, 2014).

[78] Gross domestic product is the total value of goods and services produced by the people of a nation during a year, not including income earned in foreign countries.

[79] Congressional Budget Office, Policies for Increasing Economic Growth and Employment in 2012 and 2013, statement of Douglas Elmendorf before the Committee on the Budget, United States Senate (Washington, D.C.: November 15, 2011). These multiplier estimates were based on a proposed extension of UI benefits. See also Congressional Budget Office, Estimated Impact of the American Recovery and Reinvestment Act on Employment and Economic Output from October 2012 Through December 2012 (Washington, D.C.: February 2013).

[80] Moody's Analytics, Bolstering the Economy: Helping American Families by Reauthorizing the Payroll Tax Cut and UI Benefits, testimony of Mark Zandi before the Joint Economic Committee (February 7, 2012).

[81] For example, CBO's estimates of the multiplier for UI in 2011 were generally higher than that for other categories of spending reviewed, including spending: on household assistance, such as reducing workers' payroll taxes (multiplier estimate: .1 to .9); business support, such as reducing employers' payroll taxes (multiplier estimate: .2 to 1.3); and in the form of aid to states (multiplier estimate for non-infrastructure aid: .2 to 1.0). Moody's estimate in 2012 was higher than that for all tax cuts reviewed, both for individuals and employers (multiplier estimate: .32 to 1.38), and higher than that for low-income home energy assistance (multiplier estimate: 1.13), but lower than that for Supplemental Nutrition Assistance Program benefits (multiplier estimate: 1.71).

[82] See, for example, Robert Barro, "Keynesian Economics vs. Regular Economics," Wall Street Journal, Aug. 24 2011.

[83] The Council of Economic Advisers and the Department of Labor, The Economic Benefits of Extending Unemployment Insurance (Washington, D.C.: December 2013). The Council of Economic Advisers, an agency within the Executive Office of the President, is charged with offering the President objective economic advice on domestic and international economic policy.

[84] Staff of the Chairman of the Joint Economic Committee, The Case for Maintaining Unemployment Insurance: Supporting Workers and Strengthening the Economy (Washington, D.C.: December 2011). The Joint Economic Committee is a bi-partisan, bi-cameral committee of Congress, charged with reviewing economic conditions and recommending improvements in public policy.

[85] See, for example, Jane G. Gravelle, Dynamic Scoring for Tax Legislation: A Review of Models, R43381 (Washington, D.C.: Congressional Research Service, January 24, 2014).

[86] We have previously reported that benefit reductions jeopardize the UI program's ability to stabilize the economy during recessions. See GAO, Unemployment Insurance: Program's Ability to Meet Objectives Jeopardized, GAO/HRD-93-107 (Washington, D.C.: September 28, 1993).

End Note for Appendix I

[1] Wayne Vroman, Washington's ESD Actuarial Model and The State's UI Trust Fund Balance (January 2007).

End Note for Appendix IV

[1] Wayne Vroman. Washington's ESD Actuarial Model and The State's UI Trust Fund Balance, January 2007.

End Notes for Appendix V

[1] We analyzed selected data from DOL for all states from 2006 until the middle of 2014. We excluded Illinois (which reduced maximum duration to 25 weeks for claims filed in 2012)

and Kansas (which reduced duration for weeks beginning on or after January 1, 2014, too recently to assess the effects).

[2] While a multivariate statistical analysis could, in principle, account for these additional variables, this type of analysis was beyond the scope of this report, in part because we determined that the duration reductions were too recent and the availability of emergency benefits could mitigate any effects of state policies.

[3] The civilian labor force participation rate includes those who are employed and those who are unemployed but actively looking for work. According to BLS, in January 2004, the civilian labor force participation rate was 66.1 percent. By January 2015, it had fallen to just under 63 percent. According to BLS, a major factor for the downward pressure on the labor force participation rate is the aging of the baby-boom generation. However, the decline in labor force participation is not fully explained by the aging of the population, and economists disagree about other factors that may contribute to the decline.

In: States' Reductions of Unemployment Benefits ISBN: 978-1-63483-980-8
Editor: Elias Hoffman

Chapter 2

UNEMPLOYMENT INSURANCE: CONSEQUENCES OF CHANGES IN STATE UNEMPLOYMENT COMPENSATION LAWS*

Katelin P. Isaacs

SUMMARY

This report analyzes recent changes to state Unemployment Compensation (UC) programs. Two categories of UC state law issues are considered: (1) changes in the duration of state UC unemployment benefits, and (2) changes in the UC weekly benefit amount.

Over the past several years, some states have enacted legislation to decrease the maximum number of weeks of regular state UC benefits: Until recently, all states paid at least up to 26 weeks of UC benefits to eligible, unemployed individuals. In 2011, however, six states passed legislation to decrease their maximum UC benefit durations: Arkansas, Florida, Illinois (only if certain program criteria are met across different calendar years), Michigan, Missouri, and South Carolina. In 2012, Georgia also passed legislation to decrease the maximum UC benefit duration. In 2013, Kansas and North Carolina enacted similar legislation.

Changes in UC benefit duration have consequences for the duration of federal unemployment benefits that may be available to unemployed

* This is an edited, reformatted and augmented version of a Congressional Research Service publication R41859, prepared for Members and Committees of Congress, dated August 19, 2014.

workers, including Extended Benefits (EB) and benefits from the now-expired Emergency Unemployment Compensation (EUC08) program. Since state UC benefit duration is an underlying factor in the calculation of duration for additional federal unemployment benefits, reducing UC maximum duration also reduces the number of weeks available to unemployed workers in the federal extended unemployment programs (including EUC08, which is now expired, and EB).

Prior to the expiration of the EUC08 program on December 28, 2013 (December 29, 2013, in New York), states were temporarily subject to a “nonreduction” rule (under P.L. 111-205, as amended), which made the availability of federally financed EUC08 benefits contingent on not actively changing the state’s method of calculation for UC benefits, if it would have decreased weekly benefit amounts. Some states, however, make automatic adjustments to weekly benefit amounts under existing state law. Consequently, when these states experience certain conditions, such as a decrease in the average weekly wage used in the automatic adjustment calculation, their maximum weekly UC benefit amount may have been decreased without having violated the now-expired “nonreduction” rule. P.L. 112-96 provided a specific exception to the “nonreduction” rule in the case of state legislation enacted before March 1, 2012. In February 2013, North Carolina enacted legislation that actively reduces UC weekly benefit amount calculations beginning in July 2013. Due to this violation of the “nonreduction” rule, EUC08 benefits were no longer available in North Carolina, effective June 29, 2013. All EUC08 benefits expired as of the week ending on or before January 1, 2014 (i.e., December 28, 2013; or December 29, 2013, in New York State). Any reduction to the UC weekly benefit amount also translates into reduced EB weekly benefit amounts (and EUC08 benefit amounts when the program was authorized).

Overall, the two types of changes to state UC laws and programs have consequences for the duration and amount of unemployment benefits. This report describes these changes and analyzes their consequences for UC, EUC08 (when it was authorized), and EB benefits.

Introduction

As a result of continued, high unemployment in the aftermath of the most recent recession (December 2007-June 2009), many states have enacted changes to their Unemployment Compensation (UC) programs. In general, several states are attempting to reduce the state costs of UC benefits, which are financed through state taxes on employers. This reduction in state UC benefit spending may be achieved through two types of state UC changes: (1) a reduction in the duration of state UC employment benefits and (2) a reduction in the state UC weekly benefit amount.

This report first provides a brief overview of the unemployment compensation programs and benefits that may currently be available to eligible, unemployed individuals. Next, the two categories of UC state law issues are analyzed:

1. changes in the duration of state UC unemployment benefits, and
2. changes in the maximum UC weekly benefit amount.

Overview of Unemployment Benefits

Several unemployment insurance (UI) programs may provide benefits to unemployed workers. When eligible workers lose their jobs, the UC program may provide up to 26 weeks of income support through the payment of regular state UC benefits.[1] These UC benefits may be extended in two ways. First, the permanent-law EB program may provide up to 13 or 20 weeks of additional unemployment benefits if certain economic situations exist within the state.[2] Second, until its expiration the week ending on or before January 1, 2014 (i.e., December 28, 2013; or December 29, 2013, in New York State), the temporary Emergency Unemployment Compensation (EUC08) program provided up to four tiers of additional weeks of unemployment benefits to certain workers who have exhausted their rights to UC benefits in states with high unemployment.[3]

Provided below is a brief description of the benefits available through these three UI programs: UC, EUC08 (when it was authorized), and EB.

Unemployment Compensation Program

Authorized by the Social Security Act of 1935 (SSA; P.L. 74-271), UC is a joint federal-state program that provides unemployment benefits to eligible individuals. Although federal laws and regulations provide broad guidelines on UC benefit coverage, eligibility, and benefit determination, the specifics regarding UC benefits are determined by each state. This results in essentially 53 different programs.[4] Generally, UC eligibility is based on attaining qualified wages and employment in covered work over a 12-month period (called a base period) prior to unemployment. All states require a worker to have earned a certain amount of wages or to have worked for a certain period of time (or both) within the base period to be monetarily eligible to receive any UC benefits. The methods states use to determine monetary eligibility vary greatly. Most state benefit formulas replace approximately half of a claimant's average weekly wage up to a weekly maximum. State taxes paid by employers on UC-covered wages finance UC benefits.

Maximum UC Benefit Duration

Until the recent state law changes described in this report, UC programs had been paying unemployment benefits for a maximum duration of 26 weeks. The only exceptions to the 26 week UC benefit maximum prior to these recent state law changes had been two states that provided more than 26 weeks of UC benefits (Montana: up to 28 weeks; Massachusetts: up to 30 weeks). There is nothing in federal law, however, that requires states to set their UC benefit duration maximum at 26 weeks. Thus, states have the discretion to offer fewer than 26 weeks as the maximum as well as to set their own UC benefit durations via their state UC laws. In the early decades of the UC program, there was more variation in the maximum duration of UC benefits across states, which also tended to be lower than 26 weeks. Yet since the 1960s—and until the 2011 state law changes—all states had chosen to provide up to at least 26 weeks of UC benefits to eligible individuals.[5]

Emergency Unemployment Compensation Program (now expired)

On June 30, 2008, the Supplemental Appropriations Act of 2008 (P.L. 110-252) created a new temporary, federally financed unemployment insurance program, the EUC08 program. EUC08 was the eighth federal temporary program that Congress created to extend the number of potential weeks of UC available to eligible, unemployed individuals during an economic slowdown.[6] While it was authorized, state UC agencies administered the EUC08 benefit along with regular UC benefits. Prior to expiration, EUC08 benefits were financed with general revenue from the U.S. Treasury.

The authorization for this program expired the week ending on or before January 1, 2014 (December 28, 2013; December 29, 2013, for New York).[7] There was no grandfathering of any EUC08 benefit after that date. Therefore, no EUC08 benefits are currently available.[8]

Prior to program expiration, the EUC08 benefit amount was equal to the eligible individual's weekly regular UC benefits; the following four tiers of EUC08 benefits were available:

- *Tier I* was available in all states (except North Carolina),[9] up to 14 weeks.
- *Tier II* was available in states with a TUR of at least 6% (not available in North Carolina), up to 14 weeks.[10]
- *Tier III* was available in states with a TUR of at least 7% (or an insured unemployment rate [IUR][11] of at least 4%; not available in North Carolina), up to 9 weeks.
- *Tier IV* was available in states with a TUR of at least 9% (or an IUR of at least 5%; not available in North Carolina), up to 10 weeks.

Extended Benefit Program

The Federal-State Extended Unemployment Compensation Act of 1970, P.L. 91-373, established the EB program. The EB program provides extended unemployment benefits in states that meet certain economic criteria. In all states, EB is available when a state's IUR or TUR reaches certain levels.[12]

The EB program imposes additional federal restrictions on individual eligibility for benefits beyond the state requirements for regular UC. In addition to all state requirements for regular UC eligibility, the EB program requires claimants to have at least 20 weeks of full-time insured employment or the equivalent in their base period and to conduct a systematic and sustained work search. Prior to the enactment of P.L. 112-96, states were permitted to determine which benefit, EB or EUC08, was paid first, when EUC08 was authorized.[13] Effective with P.L. 112-96, states were required to pay EUC08 benefits before EB benefits until the EUC08 program expired December 28, 2013 (December 29, 2013, in New York State).

Under permanent law, EB benefits are funded half (50%) by the federal government and half (50%) by states. The 2009 stimulus package (P.L. 111-5), as amended, temporarily changed the financing of EB benefits to be 100% federal funding through December 31, 2013.[14] (This temporary 100% federal funding for EB is now expired.) The EB benefit amount is equal to the eligible individual's weekly regular UC benefits.

There are two types of payable periods for EB benefits. First, if it meets certain state economic criteria and has certain state law trigger options in place, a state may pay EB benefits through an *EB Unemployment Period.* As discussed below, the duration of an EB Unemployment Period is based on the duration of regular UC benefits. For most states (i.e., those states with a UC maximum duration of up to 26 weeks), the EB Unemployment Period may provide up to 13 additional weeks of unemployment benefits to eligible individuals.

Second, a state may pay benefits through an *EB High Unemployment Period* if that state meets certain state economic criteria and has certain state law trigger options in place.[15] Because the duration of an EB High Unemployment Period is based on the duration of regular UC benefits in most states (i.e., those states with a UC maximum duration of up to 26 weeks), up to 20 additional weeks of EB benefits may be available to eligible individuals.

STATE LAW CHANGES TO UC BENEFIT DURATION

Regular state UC benefits are financed through state payroll taxes on employers. The state unemployment tax rate on employers in all states is "experience rated," that is, the state tax rate is based on the amount of UC paid to former employees. Generally, the more UC benefits paid to its former employees, the higher the tax rate of the employer, up to a maximum established by state law.

As a result of the most recent recession and its accompanying prolonged and high unemployment, states have paid out large amounts of UC benefits ($75.3 billion in FY2009 and $63.0 billion in FY2010 versus $30.2 billion in FY2006 and $31.4 billion in FY2007).[16] This increase in state expenditures on UC benefits has also led to large outstanding federal loans in many states[17] as well as increased employer tax rates in most states.

In response to similar state UC financial stress following prior recessions, states have typically reduced the amount of UC benefits paid to individuals through reductions in the maximum benefit amount or through changes in the underlying benefit calculations. Prior to the expiration of EUC08, however, most states were temporarily prohibited from reducing UC benefit amounts through changes to benefit calculation[18] and, therefore, acted to reduce UC benefit duration as an alternative means to decrease total UC benefit payments. Therefore, these state UC benefit duration reductions are, in part, a response to UC financial crises facing states.

At the same time, however, the duration for current federal unemployment benefits—any EB periods (and each tier of the EUC08 program when it was authorized)—are calculated based on state UC benefit duration. Thus, states that have enacted laws to reduce the duration of regular UC benefits have also reduced the duration of EB benefits (and EUC08 benefits when that program was still authorized).

Currently, there are eight states with decreased maximum UC durations in effect:

- *Arkansas* decreased its state UC maximum duration from 26 weeks to 25 weeks, effective March 30, 2011.
- *Florida* decreased the maximum UC duration from 26 weeks to a variable maximum duration, depending on the state unemployment rate and ranging from 12 weeks up to 23 weeks. Up to 12 weeks will be available if the state unemployment rate is 5% or less. Each 0.5% increase in the state unemployment rate above 5% will add an additional week of UC benefit duration. Finally, up to 23 weeks of regular UC benefits will be available if the state unemployment rate is at least 10.5%. This benefit reduction was effective January 1, 2012.
- *Georgia* decreased its UC maximum duration from 26 weeks to a variable maximum duration that ranges between 14 weeks and 20 weeks, depending on the unemployment rate in the state. A maximum UC duration of 14 weeks will be available if the state unemployment rate is 6.5% or less. Each 0.5% increase in the state unemployment rate above 6.5% will add additional weeks of UC benefit duration up to a maximum of 20 weeks of UC benefits if the state unemployment rate is at least 9%. This benefit reduction was effective May 2, 2012.
- *Kansas* decreased its UC maximum duration from 26 weeks to a variable maximum duration, using a tiered system based on the state unemployment rate. Up to 16 weeks will be available if the state unemployment rate is less than 4.5%; up to 20 weeks if the state unemployment rate is at least 4.5% and less than 6.0%; and up to 26 weeks if the state unemployment rate is at least 6.0%. This benefit reduction was effective for individuals filing an initial claim for UC benefits beginning on or after January 1, 2014.
- *Michigan* decreased its UC maximum duration from 26 weeks to 20 weeks. This change was effective for individuals filing an initial claim for UC benefits on or after January 15, 2012.
- *Missouri* decreased its UC maximum duration from 26 weeks to 20 weeks, effective April 13, 2011.

- *North Carolina* decreased the maximum UC duration from 26 weeks to a variable maximum duration, depending on the state unemployment rate and ranging from 12 weeks up to 20 weeks. Up to 12 weeks will be available if the state unemployment rate is 5.5% or less. Each 0.5% increase in the state unemployment rate above 5.5% will add an additional week of UC benefit duration. Finally, up to 20 weeks of regular UC benefits will be available if the state unemployment rate is greater than 9%. This benefit reduction is effective for individuals filing an initial claim for UC benefits on or after July 1, 2013.
- *South Carolina* also decreased its UC maximum duration from 26 weeks to 20 weeks, effective June 14, 2011.

In addition, one state enacted a law with the potential to decrease maximum UC duration if certain program criteria are met across different calendar years:

- *Illinois* enacted a law that has the potential to decrease UC maximum duration in the state (i.e., from *up to 26 weeks* down to *up to 25 weeks* or *up to 24 weeks*), depending on certain program criteria as well as calendar year. This law was effective January 1, 2012. In 2012, the program criteria were met so that only up to 25 weeks of UC benefits were available. In subsequent years, however, the required program criteria have not been met. Therefore, up to 26 weeks of UC benefits are currently available in Illinois.

Table 1 also provides details on these state changes to UC benefit duration.

Table 1. States with Unemployment Compensation (UC) Law Changes That Decrease Benefit Duration

State	State Bill or Act Number	Prior Maximum UC Duration	New Maximum UC Duration	Effective Date of New Maximum UC Duration
Arkansas	Act 861, 88th General Assembly	26 weeks	25 weeks	Effective upon enactment (March 30, 2011)

State	State Bill or Act Number	Prior Maximum UC Duration	New Maximum UC Duration	Effective Date of New Maximum UC Duration
Florida	Chapter 2011-235, Laws of Florida	26 weeks	Variable duration based on state unemployment rate:	Effective January 1, 2012
			1. 12 weeks if state unemployment rate is 5% or below 2. additional week added to 12 weeks for each 0.5% increase in state unemployment rate above 5% 3. 23 weeks if state unemployment rate is at least 10.5%	
Georgia	Act 710 (House Bill 347), Georgia General Assembly, 2011-2012 Regular Session	26 weeks	Variable duration based on state unemployment rate: 1. 14 weeks if state unemployment rate is 6.5% or below 2. additional amount added to 14 weeks for each 0.5% increase in state unemployment rate above 6.5% 3. 20 weeks if state unemployment rate is at least 9.0%	Effective May 2, 2012
Illinois	Public Act 097-0001, 97th General Assembly	26 weeks	Variable duration based on program criteria and calendar year (ranging from up to 24 weeks to up to 26 weeks)	Effective January 1, 2012
Kansas	Substitute for HB 2105	26 weeks	Variable duration by tiers based on state unemployment rate: 1. 16 weeks if state unemployment rate is less than 4.5% 2. 20 weeks if state unemployment rate is at least 4.5% but less than 6.0%	Effective for individuals filing an initial claim for UC benefits on or after January 1, 2014

Table 1. (Continued)

State	State Bill or Act Number	Prior Maximum UC Duration	New Maximum UC Duration	Effective Date of New Maximum UC Duration
			3. 26 weeks if state unemployment rate is at least 6.0%	
Michigan	Act No. 14, Public Acts of 2011	26 weeks	20 weeks	Effective for individuals filing an initial claim for UC benefits on or after January 15, 2012
Missouri	House Bill No. 163, 96th General Assembly	26 weeks	20 weeks	Effective upon enactment (April 13, 2011)
North Carolina	Session Law 2013-2, General Assembly of North Carolina, Session 2013	26 weeks	Variable duration based on state unemployment rate: 1. 12 weeks if state unemployment rate is 5.5% or below 2. additional week added to 12 weeks for each 0.5% increase in state unemployment rate above 5.5% 3. 20 weeks if state unemployment rate is greater than 9.0%	Effective July 1, 2013
South Carolina	Act No. 63, South Carolina General Assembly, 119th Session	26 weeks	20 weeks	Effective upon enactment (June 14, 2011)

Source: Compiled by the Congressional Research Service.

Consequences of Reduced UC Benefit Duration for Federal Unemployment Programs

Calculation of Benefit Duration for EUC08 Tiers (When EUC08 Was Authorized)

Prior to the expiration of EUC08, the duration of each tier of benefits was calculated through a formula based on state UC benefit duration.[19] Therefore, states that enacted laws to reduce the duration of regular UC benefits also experienced a reduction in the duration of EUC08 benefits when the program was authorized.

Specific formulas for the duration of each tier of EUC08 (when authorized) are presented below.[20] Examples of adjusted EUC08 benefit durations—based on a weekly benefit amount of $300 and a new maximum UC duration of 20 weeks—are also provided:[21]

- *Tier I* of EUC08 (prior to expiration)
    - Duration formula: 54% of the duration of an individual's total regular UC benefits in benefit year
    - Illustration of adjusted duration (formerly, the unreduced EUC08 tier I duration would have been up to 20 weeks—based on up to 26 weeks of unreduced state UC benefits—at a weekly benefit amount of $300)
        - 54% of 20 weeks of UC=10.8 weeks; up to 10 weeks at weekly benefit amount of $300 and the last week prorated at $240 ($300/0.8=$240)
- *Tier II* of EUC08 (prior to expiration)
    - Duration formula: 54% of the duration of an individual's total regular UC benefits in benefit year
    - Illustration of adjusted duration (formerly, up to 14 weeks at $300)
        - 54% of 20 weeks of UC=10.8 weeks; up to 10 weeks at weekly benefit amount of $300 and the last week prorated at $240 ($300/0.8=$240)
- *Tier III* of EUC08 (prior to expiration)
    - Duration formula: 35% of the duration of an individual's total regular UC benefits in benefit year
    - Illustration of adjusted duration (formerly, up to 13 weeks at $300)
        - 35% of 20 weeks of UC=7 weeks; up to 7 weeks at weekly benefit amount of $300

- *Tier IV* of EUC08 (prior to expiration)
    - Duration formula: 39% of the duration of an individual's total regular UC benefits in benefit year
    - Illustration of adjusted duration (formerly, up to 6 weeks at $300)
        - 39% of 20 weeks of UC=7.8 weeks; up to 7 weeks at weekly benefit amount of $300 and the last week prorated at $240 ($300/0.8=$240)

EUC08 tier duration calculations (prior to program expiration) for each state that enacted a reduction in regular UC benefit duration are provided in *Table 2.*

Calculation of Benefit Duration for EB Payable Periods

The duration of benefits for the two types of EB payable periods are set through calculations similar in structure to the calculations for EUC08 tier durations (when EUC08 was authorized).[22]

As was the case with the EUC08 program, state reductions in UC benefit durations lead to proportional reductions in the duration of the EB payable periods.

The EB payable period duration calculations and illustration of adjusted EB durations (using $300 as the weekly benefit amount and a new UC maximum duration of 20 weeks)[23] are below:

- EB Unemployment Period
    - Duration formula: 50% of the duration of individual's total regular UC benefits in benefit year
    - Illustration of adjusted duration (formerly up to 13 weeks at $300)
        - 50% of 20 weeks of UC=10 weeks; up to 10 weeks at weekly benefit amount of $300
- EB High Unemployment Period
    - Duration formula: 80% of the duration of individual's total regular UC benefits in benefit year
    - Illustration of adjusted duration (formerly up to 20 weeks at $300)
        - 80% of 20 weeks of UC=16 weeks; up to 16 weeks at weekly benefit amount of $300

Table 2 displays EB payable period duration calculations for each state that has enacted a reduction in regular UC benefit duration.

Table 2. Adjusted Maximum EUC08 (when authorized) and EB Benefit Duration Resulting from Changes to State Maximum UC Benefit Duration

State	Adjusted Maximum UC Duration	Adjusted Maximum EUC08 Tier I Duration (prior to expiration)	Adjusted Maximum EUC08 Tier II Duration (prior to expiration)	Adjusted Maximum EUC08 Tier III Duration (prior to expiration)	Adjusted Maximum EUC08 Tier IV Duration (prior to expiration)	Adjusted Maximum EB Unemployment Period Duration	Adjusted Maximum EB High Unemployment Period Duration	Effective Date for Adjusted UC Durations	Adjusted Benefit Duration Maximum from All Programs (prior to EUC08 expiration)
Arkansas	25 weeks	13 weeks and 1 week at 0.5xWBA	13 weeks and 1 week at 0.5xWBA	8 weeks and 1 week at 0.75xWBA	9 weeks and 1 week at 0.75xWBA	12 weeks and 1 week at 0.5xWBA	20 weeks	Effective 3/31/11	90.5 weeks
Florida	Variable duration based on state unemployment rate:							Effective 1/1/12	
	(1) 12 weeks if state unemployment rate is 5% or below (2) additional week added to 12 weeks for	With 12 week UC duration: 6 weeks and 1 week at 0.48xWBA	With 12 week UC duration: 6 weeks and 1 week at 0.48xWBA	With 12 week UC duration: 4 weeks and 1 week at 0.2xWBA	With 12 week UC duration: 4 weeks and 1 week at 0.68xWBA	With 12 week UC duration: 6 weeks at WBA	With 12 week UC duration: 9 weeks at WBA and 1 week at 0.6xWBA		With 12 week UC duration: 43.428 weeks

Table 2. (Continued)

State	Adjusted Maximum UC Duration	Adjusted Maximum EUC08 Tier I Duration (prior to expiration)	Adjusted Maximum EUC08 Tier II Duration (prior to expiration)	Adjusted Maximum EUC08 Tier III Duration (prior to expiration)	Adjusted Maximum EUC08 Tier IV Duration (prior to expiration)	Adjusted Maximum EB Unemployment Period Duration	Adjusted Maximum EB High Unemployment Period Duration	Effective Date for Adjusted UC Durations	Adjusted Benefit Duration Maximum from All Programs (prior to EUC08 expiration)
	each 0.5% increase in state unemployment rate above 5%								
	(3) 23 weeks if state unemployment rate is at least 10.5%	With 23 week UC duration: 12 weeks and 1 week at 0.42xWBA	With 23 week UC duration: 12 weeks and 1 week at 0.42xWBA	With 23 week UC duration: 8 weeks and 1 week at 0.05xWBA	With 23 week UC duration: 8 weeks and 1 week at 0.97xWBA	With 23 week UC duration: 11 weeks at WBA and 1 week at 0.5xWBA	With 23 week UC duration: 18 weeks at WBA and 1 week at 0.4xWBA		With 23 week UC duration: 83.26 weeks
Georgia	Variable duration based on state unemployment rate:							Effective 5/2/2012	

State	Adjusted Maximum UC Duration	Adjusted Maximum EUC08 Tier I Duration (prior to expiration)	Adjusted Maximum EUC08 Tier II Duration (prior to expiration)	Adjusted Maximum EUC08 Tier III Duration (prior to expiration)	Adjusted Maximum EUC08 Tier IV Duration (prior to expiration)	Adjusted Maximum EB Unemployment Period Duration	Adjusted Maximum EB High Unemployment Period Duration	Effective Date for Adjusted UC Durations	Adjusted Benefit Duration Maximum from All Programs (prior to EUC08 expiration)
	(1) 14 weeks if state unemployment rate is 6.5% or below	With 14 week UC duration: 7 weeks and 1 week at 0.56xWBA	With 14 week UC duration: 7 weeks and 1 week at 0.56xWBA	With 14 week UC duration: 4 weeks and 1 week at 0.9xWBA	With 14 week UC duration: 5 weeks and 1 week at 0.46xWBA	With 14 week UC duration: 7 weeks at WBA	With 14 week UC duration: 11 weeks at WBA and 1 week at 0.2xWBA		With 14 week UC duration: 50.68 weeks
	(2) additional amount added to 14 weeks for each 0.5% increase in state unemployment rate above 6.5%								

Table 2. (Continued)

State	Adjusted Maximum UC Duration	Adjusted Maximum EUC08 Tier I Duration (prior to expiration)	Adjusted Maximum EUC08 Tier II Duration (prior to expiration)	Adjusted Maximum EUC08 Tier III Duration (prior to expiration)	Adjusted Maximum EUC08 Tier IV Duration (prior to expiration)	Adjusted Maximum EB Unemployment Period Duration	Adjusted Maximum EB High Unemployment Period Duration	Effective Date for Adjusted UC Durations	Adjusted Benefit Duration Maximum from All Programs (prior to EUC08 expiration)
	(3) 20 weeks if state unemployment rate is at least 9.0%	With 20 week UC duration: 10 weeks and 1 week at 0.8xWBA	With 20 week UC duration: 10 weeks and 1 week at 0.8xWBA	With 20 week UC duration: 7 weeks	With 20 week UC duration: 7 weeks and 1 week at 0.8xWBA	With 20 week UC duration: 10 weeks	With 20 week UC duration: 16 weeks		With 20 week UC duration: 72.4weeks
Kansas	Variable duration by tiers based on state unemployment rate:							Effective for individuals filing initial claims for UC benefits on or after 1/1/14	
	(1) 16 weeks if state	With 16 week UC	With 16 week UC	With 16 week UC	With 16 week UC	With 16 week UC duration: 8	With 16 week UC duration:		With 16 week UC duration: 57.9weeks

State	Adjusted Maximum UC Duration	Adjusted Maximum EUC08 Tier I Duration (prior to expiration)	Adjusted Maximum EUC08 Tier II Duration (prior to expiration)	Adjusted Maximum EUC08 Tier III Duration (prior to expiration)	Adjusted Maximum EUC08 Tier IV Duration (prior to expiration)	Adjusted Maximum EB Unemployment Period Duration	Adjusted Maximum EB High Unemployment Period Duration	Effective Date for Adjusted UC Durations	Adjusted Benefit Duration Maximum from All Programs (prior to EUC08 expiration)
	unemployment rate is less than 4.5%	duration: 8 weeks and 1 week at 0.64xWBA	duration: 8 weeks and 1 week at 0.64xWBA	duration: 5 weeks and 1 week at 0.6xWBA	duration: 6 weeks and 1 week at 0.24xWBA	weeks	12 weeks and 1 week at 0.8xWBA		
	(2) 20 weeks if state unemployment rate is at least 4.5% but less than 6.0%	With 20 week UC duration: 10 weeks and 1 week at 0.8xWBA	With 20 week UC duration: 10 weeks and 1 week at 0.8xWBA	With 20 week UC duration: 7 weeks	With 20 week UC duration: 7 weeks and 1 week at 0.8xWBA	With 20 week UC duration: 10 weeks	With 20 week UC duration: 16 weeks		With 20 week UC duration: 72.4weeks
	(3) 26 weeks if state unemployment rate is at least 6.0%	With 26 week UC duration: 14 weeks	With 26 week UC duration: 14 weeks	With 26 week UC duration: 9 weeks	With 26 week UC duration: 10 weeks	With 26 week UC duration: 13 weeks	With 26 week UC duration: 20 weeks		With 26 week UC duration: 93 weeks
Michigan	20 weeks	10 weeks and 1 week at 0.8xWBA	10 weeks and 1 week at 0.8xWBA	With 20 week UC duration: 7 weeks	With 20 week UC duration: 7 weeks and 1 week at	10 weeks	16 weeks	Effective for individuals filing initial	72.4 weeks

Table 2. (Continued)

State	Adjusted Maximum UC Duration	Adjusted Maximum EUC08 Tier I Duration (prior to expiration)	Adjusted Maximum EUC08 Tier II Duration (prior to expiration)	Adjusted Maximum EUC08 Tier III Duration (prior to expiration)	Adjusted Maximum EUC08 Tier IV Duration (prior to expiration)	Adjusted Maximum EB Unemployment Period Duration	Adjusted Maximum EB High Unemployment Period Duration	Effective Date for Adjusted UC Durations	Adjusted Benefit Duration Maximum from All Programs (prior to EUC08 expiration)
					0.8xWBA			claims for UC benefits on or after 1/15/12	
Missouri	20 weeks	10 weeks and 1 week at 0.8xWBA	10 weeks and 1 week at 0.8xWBA	With 20 week UC duration: 7 weeks	With 20 week UC duration: 7 weeks and 1 week at 0.8xWBA	10 weeks	16 weeks	Effective 4/13/11	72.4 weeks
North Carolina	Variable duration based on state unemployment rate:							Effective for individuals filing initial claims for UC benefits on or after 7/1/13	
	(1) 12 weeks if state unemployment rate is	NA	NA	NA	NA	With 12 week UC duration: 6 weeks at WBA	With 12 week UC duration: 9 weeks at		With 12 week UC duration: 21.6weeks

State	Adjusted Maximum UC Duration	Adjusted Maximum EUC08 Tier I Duration (prior to expiration)	Adjusted Maximum EUC08 Tier II Duration (prior to expiration)	Adjusted Maximum EUC08 Tier III Duration (prior to expiration)	Adjusted Maximum EUC08 Tier IV Duration (prior to expiration)	Adjusted Maximum EB Unemployment Period Duration	Adjusted Maximum EB High Unemployment Period Duration	Effective Date for Adjusted UC Durations	Adjusted Benefit Duration Maximum from All Programs (prior to EUC08 expiration)
	5.5% or below						WBA and 1 week at 0.6xWBA		
	(2) additional week added to 12 weeks for each 0.5% increase in state unemployment rate above 5.5%								
	(3) 20 weeks if state unemployment rate is greater than 9.0%	NA	NA	NA	NA	With 20 week UC duration: 10 weeks	With 20 week UC duration: 16 weeks		With 20 week UC duration: 36weeks

Table 2. (Continued)

State	Adjusted Maximum UC Duration	Adjusted Maximum EUC08 Tier I Duration (prior to expiration)	Adjusted Maximum EUC08 Tier II Duration (prior to expiration)	Adjusted Maximum EUC08 Tier III Duration (prior to expiration)	Adjusted Maximum EUC08 Tier IV Duration (prior to expiration)	Adjusted Maximum EB Unemployment Period Duration	Adjusted Maximum EB High Unemployment Period Duration	Effective Date for Adjusted UC Durations	Adjusted Benefit Duration Maximum from All Programs (prior to EUC08 expiration)
South Carolina	20 weeks	10 weeks and 1 week at 0.8xWBA	10 weeks and 1 week at 0.8xWBA	With 20 week UC duration: 7 weeks	With 20 week UC duration: 7 weeks and 1 week at 0.8xWBA	10 weeks	16 weeks	Effective 6/14/11	72.4 weeks

Source: Compiled by Congressional Research Service.

Notes: The authorization for the EUC08 program expired the week ending on or before January 1, 2014. Consequently, EUC08 benefits were available through December 28, 2013 (December 29, 2013, for New York). Adjusted maximum EUC08 benefit durations and adjusted maximum durations from all programs reflect EUC08 benefits authorized prior to this expiration.

WBA: weekly benefit amount. All weeks of benefits are paid out in terms of full WBA unless a pro-rated WBA calculation is provided. States were authorized to augment pro-rated weeks of EUC08 tiers with amounts from subsequent EUC08 tiers in order to bring payments up to the full weekly benefit amount (Employment and Training Administration, U.S. Department of Labor, "Emergency Unemployment Compensation, 2008—Questions and Answers," Unemployment Insurance Program Letter 23-08, Change 3, December 24, 2008, http://wdr.doleta.gov/directives/attach/UIPL/UIPL23-08C3.pdf). The "Adjusted Benefit Duration Maximum from All Programs" column sums the total weeks from all four tiers of EUC08 and an EB High Unemployment Period, including full weeks of WBA and pro-rated weeks of WBA.

Illinois is not listed in this table since there is no UC maximum duration reduction effective in IL currently.

NA: not available. Due to a violation of the "nonreduction" rule (under P.L. 111-205, as amended), the EUC08 agreement between North Carolina and the Secretary of the U.S. Department of Labor was terminated. All tiers of EUC08 ended in North Carolina as of June 29, 2013.

The adjusted maximum benefit durations listed in the table for EUC08 and EB (and the maximum duration from all programs, which had previously been 93 weeks) apply to beneficiaries who file an initial claim for UC benefits after the effective date for adjusted UC durations. Individuals who received or are receiving UC benefits prior to the effective date for the state reduction in maximum UC benefits maintain the previous, unreduced UC, EUC08, and EB benefit durations. The EUC08 benefit duration formulas provided in this table were effective prior to EUC08 expiration. For more details, see CRS Report R42444, Emergency Unemployment Compensation (EUC08): Status of Benefits Prior to Expiration, by Katelin P. Isaacs and Julie M. Whittaker.

States with Reduced Weekly Benefit Amounts

P.L. 110-252, as amended, included a "nonreduction" rule that made the availability of federally financed EUC08 benefits (when authorized) contingent on not actively changing the state's method of calculation for UC benefits, if the method would have decreased weekly benefit amounts. This "nonreduction" rule was a condition of the EUC08 federal-state agreement prior to EUC08 expiration. In general, states were not permitted to pay an average weekly UC benefit amount that is less than what would have been paid under state law prior to what was in effect as of June 2, 2010, and still be able to pay EUC08 benefits.[24] However, states could reduce weekly benefits if that reduction happens automatically in certain circumstances as required by a state law that was in place before the enactment of P.L. 111-5. Any reduction to the UC weekly benefit amount also translates into reduced EUC08 (when authorized) and EB weekly benefit amounts.

Prior to P.L. 110-252, 36 states had enacted state laws that calculate the maximum weekly UC benefit via *automatic* adjustments based on the average weekly wage in a state.[25] Therefore, if the average weekly wage declines in these states, they may experience automatic reductions in UC average weekly benefit amount, which are permitted under the "nonreduction" rule. For instance, in 2011, New Jersey and Oklahoma appear to have met these conditions and to have experienced automatic reductions in their state UC weekly benefit amount. Similarly, in 2012, Hawaii also seems to have met the necessary conditions to automatically reduce the state UC weekly benefit amount.[26]

P.L. 112-96 provided a specific exception to this UC "nonreduction" rule in the case of state legislation that was enacted before March 1, 2012. States that made changes to the regular UC benefit amount prior to March 1, 2012, were not subject to the "nonreduction" rule.

In February 2013, North Carolina enacted legislation that included a provision to actively reduce UC weekly benefit amounts in the state. Effective on or after July 1, 2013, this state law provision violated the "nonreduction" rule and, therefore, terminated the EUC08 agreement between North Carolina and the Secretary of the U.S. Department of Labor. All tiers of EUC08 ended in North Carolina as of June 29, 2013.[27] With the expiration of the EUC08 program as of the week ending on or before January 1, 2014 (i.e., December 28, 2013; or December 29, 2013, in New York State), the "nonreduction" rule is no longer effective.

Any state UC benefit reductions also reduce weekly amounts for EB benefits (and EUC08 benefits when authorized), which are paid out in the same amount. Only individuals filing new state UC claims after the effective date for reduced UC durations, however, would experience reductions in UC, EUC08 (when authorized), or EB benefits.

End Notes

[1] Or, in the case of the states described in the report section on "State Law Changes to UC Benefit Duration," UC currently pays fewer than up to 26 weeks.

[2] See report section on "Calculation of Benefit Duration for EB Payable Periods" for the calculation of EB benefit durations in states that have reduced regular UC benefit duration.

[3] See report section on "Calculation of Benefit Duration for EUC08 Tiers" for the calculation of EUC08 benefit durations prior to EUC08 expiration in states with reduced regular UC benefit durations. In states without UC duration reductions up to 47 weeks of total EUC08 benefits was generally available prior to EUC08 expiration in certain states with high unemployment. For more details on the structure and availability of EUC08 benefits, see CRS Report R42444, Emergency Unemployment Compensation (EUC08): Status of Benefits Prior to Expiration, by Katelin P. Isaacs and Julie M. Whittaker.

[4] The District of Columbia, Puerto Rico, and the Virgin Islands are considered to be states in UC law.

[5] Puerto Rico is an exception to this pattern of state convergence on 26 weeks as the maximum UC benefit duration in the 1960s. When it originally entered the federal-state UC system in 1961, Puerto Rico provided a lower maximum UC benefit duration (i.e., up to 16 weeks in 1961 and then up to 20 weeks for most of the 1970-1990 period). Puerto Rico did not provide up to 26 weeks of UC benefits until 1991. For more information on state UC benefit duration, including changes over time, see DOL's "Significant Provisions of State UI Laws," available at http://www.workforcesecurity. doleta.gov/unemploy/statelaws.asp# sigprouilaws.

[6] The other programs became effective in 1958, 1961, 1972, 1975, 1982, 1991, and 2002. See CRS Report RL34340, Extending Unemployment Compensation Benefits During Recessions, by Julie M. Whittaker and Katelin P. Isaacs.

[7] The EUC08 program has been amended 11 times (P.L. 110-449, P.L. 111-5, P.L. 111-92, P.L. 111-118, P.L. 111-144, P.L. 111-157, P.L. 111-205, P.L. 111-312, P.L. 112-78, P.L. 112-96, and P.L. 112-240). For more details on EUC08, including its legislative history, see CRS Report R42444, Emergency Unemployment Compensation (EUC08): Status of Benefits Prior to Expiration, by Katelin P. Isaacs and Julie M. Whittaker.

[8] Effective on or after July 1, 2013, EUC08 benefits were no longer available in North Carolina. North Carolina enacted legislation in February 2013 that included a provision to actively reduce UC weekly benefit amounts in the state. This state law provision violated the "nonreduction" rule and, therefore, terminated the EUC08 agreement between North Carolina and the Secretary of the U.S. Department of Labor.

[9] See previous footnote. North Carolina terminated its EUC08 agreement on July 1, 2013.

[10] The TUR (the total unemployment rate) is the seasonally-adjusted, three-month average of the ratio of unemployed workers to all workers (employed and unemployed) in the labor market.

[11] The IUR (the insured unemployment rate) is the ratio of UC claimants divided by individuals in UC-covered jobs.

[12] DOL's weekly trigger notices for the EB program are available online at http://www.workforcesecurity.doleta.gov/ unemploy/claims_arch.asp.

[13] Alaska was the only state to pay EB benefits first when this option was available under P.L. 110-252, as amended.

[14] This temporary 100% federal financing of EB benefits did not include "non-sharable" benefits (generally, these are former state and local employees' EB benefits).

[15] Ibid.

[16] For more details on revenues and expenditures associated with UC benefits, see CRS Report RL33362, Unemployment Insurance: Programs and Benefits, by Julie M. Whittaker and Katelin P. Isaacs.

[17] For more details on federal loans to states to pay UC benefits, see CRS Report RS22954, The Unemployment Trust Fund (UTF): State Insolvency and Federal Loans to States, by Julie M. Whittaker.

[18] For a fuller discussion of this issue, including details on states that have been able to reduce weekly UC benefit amounts, see the report section on "States with Reduced Weekly Benefit Amounts."

[19] Prior to program expiration, the duration of benefits for each tier of EUC08 (as well as any EB payable period) was set through calculations based on the lesser of (1) the state benefit criteria, which is a set percentage of the duration of regular UC benefits (e.g., 54% of the individual's total regular UC duration in a benefit year for Tier I of EUC08 prior to expiration) or (2) the maximum weekly amount criteria, which is the multiple of an individual's average weekly benefit amount under the UC program (e.g., 13 times an individual's average weekly benefit amount in a benefit year for Tier I of EUC08 prior to expiration). In the event of state reduction in UC benefit durations, the former calculation—the state benefit criteria—would be lower and, thus, applicable. Therefore, this report's discussion of the benefit duration calculation for all tiers of EUC08 (when authorized) and all payable periods of EB focuses on this state benefit criteria formula in its explanations and illustrations of duration calculations.

[20] These EUC08 benefit duration formulas were effective for EUC08 tiers prior to expiration. The structure and availability of EUC08 tiers changed several times since the initial EUC08 program authorization. For more details on this legislative history, see CRS Report R42444, Emergency Unemployment Compensation (EUC08): Status of Benefits Prior to Expiration, by Katelin P. Isaacs and Julie M. Whittaker.

[21] The average weekly benefit amount was $315—or roughly $300—across all states as of July 2014 (DOL). Michigan, Missouri, and South Carolina have enacted state laws to reduce their maximum UC benefit duration to 20 weeks.

[22] See footnote 19 for more technical details.

[23] See footnote 21 for rationale behind these data points.

[24] This "nonreduction" rule was put into place when P.L. 111-205 amended P.L. 110-252. There was a similar, but programmatically distinct "nonreduction" rule in P.L. 111-5, as amended, which prevented states from actively changing the method of calculation of the UC weekly benefit amount to pay UC benefit amounts less than what would have been paid under state law prior to December 31, 2008. No states acted to decrease UC benefit amounts between

December 31, 2008, and June 2, 2010, when the federal authorization for this earlier "nonreduction" rule expired.

[25] The 36 states that calculate benefit amounts using automatic adjustments under prior state law are Arkansas, Colorado, Connecticut, District of Columbia, Hawaii, Idaho, Illinois, Iowa, Kansas, Kentucky, Louisiana, Maine, Massachusetts, Minnesota, Montana, Nevada, New Jersey, New Mexico, North Carolina, North Dakota, Ohio, Oklahoma, Oregon, Pennsylvania, Puerto Rico, Rhode Island, South Carolina, South Dakota, Texas, Utah, Vermont, Virgin Islands, Washington, West Virginia, Wisconsin, and Wyoming.
These 36 states could experience reductions in UC weekly benefit amounts under the "nonreduction" rule if (1) the average weekly wages in states declined and the corresponding methods of calculation formula resulted in a benefit decrease (for specific information regarding these state-specific methods of benefit calculation, see DOL's "Comparison of State Unemployment Laws, 2013," Chapter 3: Monetary Eligibility, Table 3.6, pp. 13-15, available at http://www.workforcesecurity.doleta. gov/unemp loy/pdf/uilaw compar/2013/monetary.pdf) and (2) the state did not otherwise prevent this benefit amount reduction through enactment of new state legislation.

[26] See DOL's "Significant Provisions of State UI Laws," available at http://www.work forcesecurity.doleta.gov/ unemploy/statelaws.asp.

[27] See U.S. Department of Labor, EUC08 Trigger Notice No. 2013-24, effective June 30, 2013, http://www.workforcesecurity.doleta.gov/ unemploy/euc_trigger/2013/euc_063013.html; and North Carolina Department of Commerce, Division of Employment Security, "Unemployment Insurance Law Changes—Claimants Questions and Answers," http://www.ncesc1.com/individual/2013LawChangeQA.asp.

INDEX

A

adjustment, 14, 61, 68
advisory body, 56
age, 59
agencies, 3, 36, 44, 70
aggregate demand, 32, 33
Alaska, 58, 90
algorithm, 40
American Recovery and Reinvestment Act, 8, 34, 56, 59, 61, 63
American Recovery and Reinvestment Act of 2009, 8, 34, 56, 59, 61
Appropriations Act, 8, 70
assessment, 50, 56
attachment, 5, 43
audit, 5, 44
authority, 58
avoidance, 47

B

base, 10, 17, 18, 50, 59, 61, 69, 71
behavioral change, 63
behaviors, 56
benchmarking, 43, 51
beneficiaries, 36, 87
bond market, 59
bonds, 18, 50, 61
BTC, 61
Bureau of Labor Statistics, 1, 5, 21, 37, 39
business cycle, 10

C

causation, 27
Census, 27, 62
Chad, 38
challenges, 5
cluster analysis, 37, 39, 44, 59
clustering, 40
clusters, 39, 40
commercial, 50
compensation, 6, 8, 25, 63, 69
composition, 16, 39, 40, 44, 59
Congress, 1, 8, 32, 36, 56, 63, 64, 67, 70
Congressional Budget Office, 1, 3, 32, 34, 43, 63
construction, 40
consumption, 27
convergence, 89
cost, 1, 3, 12, 17, 28, 29, 30, 32, 36, 38, 44, 45, 49, 58, 59, 61
cost saving, 17, 30, 38, 49, 61
covering, 59
credentials, 50
criminal acts, 57
crises, 72

D

data set, 44
Democratic Party, 60
Department of Commerce, 91
Department of Labor (DOL), vii, 1, 2, 3, 5, 6, 7, 8, 11, 12, 14, 24, 25, 30, 32, 31, 33, 35, 36, 37, 39, 41, 43, 44, 45, 46, 47, 49, 50, 52, 53, 54, 56, 57, 58, 59, 61, 64, 89, 90, 91
Department of the Treasury, 15, 44, 56, 60
directives, 86
directors, 21, 26, 56
disability, 27
District of Columbia, 5, 40, 56, 89, 91
diversity, 38
draft, 36, 38, 57
drawing, 61

E

earnings, 4, 6, 7, 18, 57
economic downturn, 6, 8, 10, 32, 35, 36
economic efficiency, 26
economic indicator, 27
economic policy, 64
economics, 15
eligibility criteria, 7
emergency, 8, 9, 10, 16, 23, 24, 25, 29, 33, 50, 57, 58, 61, 63, 65
employees, 12, 72, 90
employers, 6, 10, 11, 14, 17, 18, 33, 50, 58, 59, 60, 61, 64, 68, 70, 72
employment, 7, 18, 20, 23, 26, 27, 32, 33, 34, 40, 41, 43, 57, 61, 63, 69, 71
energy, 64
enrollment, 26
ESD, 64
ethnicity, 59
evidence, 5, 44, 57
expenditures, 72, 90

F

families, 27
federal assistance, 32, 36
federal government, vii, 2, 3, 4, 5, 6, 8, 10, 11, 27, 28, 29, 30, 31, 32, 35, 36, 49, 56, 58, 59, 62, 71
federal law, 4, 18, 22, 25, 29, 37, 56, 60, 61, 69, 70
Federal Reserve, 62
financial, 2, 24, 35, 72
financial relief, 35
fiscal policy, 58
fiscal year, 36, 58
flexibility, 6, 7, 11, 35
food, 27
force, 26, 27, 53, 55, 65
formula, 10, 77, 78, 90, 91
fraud, 18
funding, 8, 34, 36, 41, 58, 71
funds, 6, 11, 16, 18

G

GAO, 1, 2, 3, 7, 9, 11, 12, 14, 20, 21, 22, 23, 24, 25, 29, 31, 33, 34, 39, 41, 43, 45, 46, 47, 48, 49, 50, 51, 52, 53, 54, 55, 57, 58, 59, 60, 61, 63, 64
GDP, 1, 32, 33
Georgia, 2, 4, 5, 17, 19, 20, 21, 25, 30, 31, 38, 39, 40, 42, 44, 46, 47, 48, 49, 52, 56, 60, 61, 62, 63, 67, 73, 75, 80
goods and services, 63
government spending, 33, 34
governments, 62
governor, 38, 62
grant programs, 58
Great Recession, 63
gross domestic product, 1, 32
guidelines, 69

H

Hawaii, 46, 60, 88, 91

health, 16
history, 7, 18, 57, 89, 90
homogeneity, 13, 40, 59, 62
House, 75, 76

I

ideal, 26
illegal drug use, 56
improvements, 64
incidence, 27
income, 32, 35, 40, 60, 63, 64, 69
income support, 69
individual character, 39
individual characteristics, 39
individuals, vii, 2, 3, 4, 5, 6, 7, 18, 19, 21, 23, 24, 26, 27, 32, 35, 37, 38, 41, 43, 53, 56, 62, 64, 69, 70, 72, 73, 74, 75, 76, 82, 83, 84, 89, 90
industry, 39, 40, 59
inflation, 43
infrastructure, 64
institutions, 33
integrity, 17, 18, 61
internal controls, 5, 44
investment, 33
Iowa, 58, 91
issues, 62, 67, 69

J

jobless, 26
Joint Economic Committee, 33, 63, 64

K

Keynesian, 64

L

labor force, 5, 11, 21, 26, 27, 41, 43, 55, 59, 65
labor force participation, 11, 26, 65
labor market, 26, 90
laws, 10, 37, 68, 70, 73, 77
layoffs, 11
lead, 27, 35, 78
legislation, 8, 50, 61, 67, 68, 88, 89, 91
light, 26
loans, 3, 11, 12, 13, 15, 17, 18, 39, 44, 45, 59, 61, 72, 90
logging, 40
Louisiana, 91

M

magnitude, 5, 30, 32, 38, 55
majority, 12
manufacturing, 40
Maryland, 46
matrix, 40
median, 13, 15, 45, 60
Medicaid, 34, 59
membership, 13, 15, 40
mental health, 62
methodology, 5
Mexico, 91
Missouri, 2, 4, 5, 7, 20, 21, 25, 30, 31, 39, 40, 42, 44, 46, 47, 49, 52, 53, 58, 60, 62, 63, 67, 73, 76, 84, 90
models, 26, 33
modifications, 36
Montana, 57, 70, 91
multiplier, 32, 33, 34, 43, 63, 64
multiplier effect, 32, 33, 34

N

NPR, 62

O

officials, 5, 7, 13, 16, 17, 18, 19, 21, 24, 37, 38, 42, 43, 47, 48, 49, 50, 51, 52, 56, 57, 60, 61, 62
Oklahoma, 88, 91

Organization for Economic Cooperation and Development, 62
oversight, 6

P

payroll, 33, 59, 64, 72
penalties, 18, 57
policy, 3, 5, 32, 35, 38, 39, 42, 43
policy responses, 3
population, 11, 15, 39, 40, 41, 42, 59, 61, 62, 63, 65
population size, 42
poverty, 26, 27, 43
poverty reduction, 43
President, 36, 56, 64
private sector, 33
probability, 37, 42
program administration, 6
project, 24, 42, 51
public policy, 64
Puerto Rico, 56, 89, 91

R

race, 59
recession, 2, 4, 5, 6, 11, 12, 13, 14, 15, 19, 26, 27, 32, 35, 38, 41, 53, 54, 55, 56, 58, 62, 68, 72
recommendations, 2, 36, 43
recovery, 2, 4, 8, 11, 26, 35, 38, 55, 56
regulations, 4, 12, 37, 59, 69
reliability, 5, 43
relief, 12, 35, 59
Republican Party, 60
requirement(s), 6, 7, 16, 18, 50, 51, 56, 57, 58, 60, 61, 71
researchers, 5, 43
reserves, 3, 6, 10, 11, 12, 14, 58
resources, 13, 15, 38, 40, 44, 45, 62
response, 18, 72
restoration, 35
restrictions, 56, 61, 71
revenue, 10, 11, 12, 17, 70
rights, 69
risk, 14, 26
rules, 3, 10, 18, 58

S

safety, 26
savings, 17, 28, 30, 49, 61, 62
school, 33
scope, 56, 65
Senate, 4, 63
showing, 33
signals, 20
simulation, 24
Social Security, 1, 6, 27, 43, 57, 69
Social Security Disability Insurance, 27, 43
South Dakota, 46, 58, 91
spending, 26, 32, 33, 34, 35, 64, 68
SSA, 69
stabilization, 32
stabilizers, 35
stakeholders, 14, 26, 37, 38, 60
standardization, 40
state laws, 2, 4, 7, 12, 16, 17, 21, 37, 48, 49, 50, 56, 88, 90
state legislatures, 60
statistics, 41
stimulus, 3, 32, 34, 35, 71
stress, vii, 2, 72
structure, 38, 78, 89, 90
suboptimal employment, 26
Supplemental Nutrition Assistance Program, 27, 64
survival, 37, 42
survival rate, 37, 42

T

target, 12, 49, 61
tax base, 6
tax collection, 52
tax cuts, 14, 64
tax increase, 17, 61
tax rates, 11, 12, 14, 17, 41, 52, 60, 61, 72

tax system, 59
taxation, 10
taxes, 3, 6, 10, 13, 14, 17, 18, 33, 34, 52, 58, 59, 61, 62, 64, 68, 70, 72
taxpayers, 34
technical change, 37
technical comments, 36
Title I, 57
Title IV, 57
transportation, 34
Treasury, 40, 45, 60
triggers, 12, 48
trust fund, 2, 10, 12, 13, 14, 15, 17, 19, 24, 38, 39, 41, 43, 44, 45, 46, 47, 49, 50, 51, 52, 58, 59, 60, 61, 62, 64, 90
trust funds, 13, 15, 41, 49, 58, 59, 61

U

U.S. Department of Labor, 59, 86, 87, 88, 89, 91
U.S. Treasury, 70
unemployed individuals, 24, 35, 67, 69, 70
unemployment insurance, vii, 1, 2, 4, 8, 35, 36, 37, 58, 69, 70
unemployment rate, 2, 6, 7, 10, 11, 13, 15, 17, 19, 20, 27, 38, 39, 41, 43, 48, 54, 55, 57, 60, 61, 62, 71, 73, 74, 75, 76, 79, 80, 81, 82, 83, 84, 85, 90
United States, v, 1, 4, 53, 54, 62, 63
Urban Institute, 38, 42, 51, 62
UWC, 58

V

variables, 37, 39, 40, 41, 51, 56, 59, 62, 65

W

wages, 10, 12, 14, 15, 18, 41, 57, 59, 60, 69, 91
Washington, 5, 18, 19, 24, 38, 39, 42, 45, 51, 52, 56, 57, 58, 59, 61, 62, 63, 64, 91
weakness, 60
websites, 43
Wisconsin, 46, 47, 91
workers, vii, 2, 6, 8, 26, 27, 33, 58, 62, 64, 68, 69, 90
workforce, 5, 38, 39
working conditions, 57